IN PURSUIT OF MUSICAL EXCELLENCE

IN PURSUIT OF MUSICAL EXCELLENCE

Essays On Musicality

John Yarrington

PENIEL UNLIMITED

Published 2021 PENIEL UNLIMITED, LLC

Dr. Michael Marcades, Founding President / Executive Editor
Kelly Marcades, CFO / Marketing Director
321 Avalanche Avenue
Georgetown, Texas 78626
https://www.penielunlimited.com
michaelmarcades@gmail.com

ISBN: 978-0-578-94528-6

Cover Design by Daniel Whisnant
https://www.suissemade.com

Copyright © 2021 by John Yarrington

All rights reserved. No part of this book may be reproduced in any manner whatsoever without written permission except in the case of brief quotations embodied in critical articles and reviews.

First Printing, 2021

DEDICATION

IN PURSUIT OF MUSICAL EXCELLENCE:
Essays on Musicality

"God gave you breath, and that's about all you get,"
explains the former singer whose own professional career was
cut short by chronic lung problems she blames on
a childhood around the steel mills of Campbell, Ohio.
"You get breath for nothing, but everything else
you ought to work for."
* Betty Campbell, President Emeritus, Harlem School of the Arts
(*New York Times, Sunday, January 25, 1995*)

Music is in continual dialogue with us,
dispensing its silent and abstract aural wisdom to us;
and to lifelong musicians. Music always knows more
about us than we can ever know about it.
* Patrick Summers, *The Spirit of this Place*

Music is a spiritual practice
for no other reason but that it
organizes silence, and it shares many
qualities with spiritual practice.
* Patrick Summers, *The Spirit of this Place*

* * *

Dedicated to my wife, Diane, my fiercest critic
and my strongest supporter.

REVIEW COMMENTARY...

Craig Hella Johnson - *Conspirare*, Artistic Director; Cincinnati Vocal Arts Ensemble; Music Director; Texas State University, Artist in Residence; Victoria Bach Festival, Conductor Emeritus

While reading John Yarrington's *In Pursuit of Musical Excellence: Essays on Musicality*, I had the feeling of being in conversation with both a wise and wonderful friend and an inspirational teacher. It is clear on every page that these are the words of one who has dedicated his life to the choral craft. His talent, imagination and skills were shaped by a powerful lineage of legendary choral leaders and he now stands among them with his own distinctive voice and significant contributions to offer. He plays host to these choral luminaries along with several other important cultural voices by including many impactful quotations and unpublished notes. He writes both about the inspirational and the practical, always with a keen eye to eliminating anything in our work or process that is not essential in order that we may ultimately attempt to reveal the essence of a work. In the introduction, John writes, "I read constantly to be renewed, to be reminded, to be encouraged." In reading this collection of essays, I was consistently renewed, reminded and encouraged in many ways about this sacred and ennobling craft of choral music. I enjoyed this book immensely and I am deeply grateful for John Yarrington and for his outstanding contributions to our field.

Hilary Apfelstadt, PhD. - Professor Emerita of Conducting at the University of Toronto, Canada; Interim Executive Director of the American Choral Directors Association (ACDA), 2020 - 2021

Author John Yarrington has amassed great wisdom in a career that spans more than 50 years working with choral ensembles in communities, churches, and universities. He presents his observations and those of some of his mentors and col-

REVIEW COMMENTARY . . .

leagues in a practical, direct manner, with no words wasted. In Chapter 6 we read, "You are beginning to get the focus of this book: what is not efficient needs to be eliminated." Whether that refers to words, gestures, or actions, we also learn that "singing is relational," and that as conductors, we need to care for the music makers, just as we care for the music itself. There are practical rehearsal strategies, discussions of musical examples, advice about programming and the importance of text, about working with instrumentalists, and about being true to the music, among other concepts. Chapter 1 mostly comprises a series of quotations from musicians and each of these would serve as the basis for an excellent discussion in itself.

This book would serve as valuable reading material for prospective conductors and seasoned musicians who would benefit from practical reminders, delivered in a kind and sometimes humorous way. Yarrington knows the field intimately, having dedicated his life to choral music. One can trust these words. I highly recommend this book.

CONTENTS

DEDICATION v
REVIEW COMMENTARY... vii
INTRODUCTION: IN THE BEGINNING WAS THE WORD xi

1 | An Approach to Music and the Purpose of Analysis   1

2 | The Interpretation Myth   17

3 | Vocal Athletes   27

4 | Rehearsal Strategies   35

5 | Understanding Articulation – the Long and Short of It   43

6 | The Energy Mystique   48

7 | Already Too Loud!   56

8 | The Relationship Quotient   67

9 | Why Making Music Matters   74

EPILOGUE 79
BIBLIOGRAPHY 83
THE AUTHOR 85

INTRODUCTION: IN THE BEGINNING WAS THE WORD

In the beginning was the word.
The music was in that word.
The music set that word singing.

In the beginning was a sound – balanced, in tune, on an active breath, with released jaw, shoulders down and head balanced on spine – a sound from a fully aligned body. In the beginning was choice. Choice of a worthy text (words) for which the music is vehicle and champion.

In the beginning were the questions ABOUT this choice:

1. What kind of TEXT are you? Do you have enough strength and value to sustain repeated encounters? Will you stand up to scrutiny? Do your words matter?
2. What kind of MUSIC are you? Do you have brothers or sisters? Who are your people? What forces (vocal or instrumental) are required?

In the beginning was careful, systematic study viewed through the lens of historical setting and performance practice, of form and structure, of theory and harmony.

INTRODUCTION: IN THE BEGINNING WAS THE WORD

In the beginning was the ensemble: building a vehicle through which the word may be heard with clarity, precision, accuracy, beauty, and through which individuals are drawn together to do something rather extraordinary which, by themselves, they could not accomplish in the same way nor with the same results.

In the beginning was the care and nurture of the ensemble, caring for the music equally with care for the music makers.

In the beginning was an atmosphere which expects the utmost from each individual music maker, including responsibility for all of the technical musical components (breath/vowels/consonants/articulation) aligned with the terrific responsibility for what comes out of each individual mouth, heart and mind.

In the beginning was a gesture which calls forth effectively and economically from this ensemble, the highest form of our art. This gesture never detracts from, but always is in the service of, the music. This gesture calls forth from the music makers the totality of, the sum of, every voice, heart and mind in the room. The gesture is welcoming, evoking, and never dictatorial.

So, do we really need another book about choral music in any shape or form?

Another book about musical concepts of interpretation, phrasing, gesture, style, ensemble building, rehearsal planning, working with instrumentalists, cares and concerns of working with people? Hasn't enough been said about these areas?

I am reminded about the story of the conductor who, after repeated attempts to clean up a particular part, was asked: "Can the altos HEAR the bottom of page 10?"

His response: "Obviously not!"

So, my response to the question about enough being said is: obviously not. Hence this book.

INTRODUCTION: IN THE BEGINNING WAS THE WORD

I read constantly to be renewed, to be reminded, and to be re-encouraged. I am renewed when I encounter a different perspective, or reminded when someone espouses concepts I also value. And I am re-encouraged to know that others are on a constant journey to make real a musical experience which understands and values the music but also understands and values the music maker.

The word "pursuit" or "pursue" offers several important definitions:
a. To strive to gain; seek to attain or accomplish
b. To carry on (a course of action, train of thoughts)
c. To practice (an occupation, pastime)
d. To follow (a path)
e. To continue on one's way; go on with or continue (a journey)

So, to "pursue" musical excellence seems to be right in line with these definitions. I know, for instance, that there are new readers. I have seen students at Houston Baptist University who need to know the basics of our art and craft. They need to know "standard" literature and often are woefully inadequate in this important area. At workshops I experience the same hunger for the tools and literature for the musical excellence we all want. Young conductors especially lack the experience they can only gain out "in the field." However, many go unprepared with what I consider to be the basics: how to look at a score (bringing to bear everything learned in history, literature, theory) so that one knows where to begin, how to proceed, and which gestures will bring results. There is the important area of vocal technique, quite different from the vocal studio experience.

Do I have anything to add to the current literature? I believe I do. I have spent a lifetime with volunteer singers in church, teaching a wide variety of literature, pushing the proverbial envelope, challenging "them" to sing better, more musically (beautifully) and to respond to basic gestures where "they" have responsibility for the outcome. I do not find this very different than in the school setting where I served for eighteen years at HBU and now at The University of St. Thomas.

I remember that first youth choir at McFarlin United Memorial Methodist Church in Norman, Oklahoma, over fifty years ago. A room full of teenagers with a sound, best described as breathy, weak and unfocused. That is a kind definition. I had to learn how to develop a healthy sound, full of life and color, and appropriate to the literature being sung. Not to mention that area of vocal change with its own set of problems. All in all, a terrific learning experience for a young conductor.

At Mcfarlin United Methodist Church, I was fortunate to have close proximity to the University of Oklahoma and its resources. I was able to perform major works with the church choir and instrumentalists, including Handel *Messiah,* Bach *St. John Passion,* Bach *St. Matthew Passion,* Vaughan Williams *Hodie,* and the Britten *St. Nicolas.* The cellist at the university, Marge Cornelius, taught me much about working with orchestra and I am forever indebted to her.

What did I learn? Not to talk but to listen. To allow the players to play through without stopping to see the entirety of the program. Not to be concerned at the outset about balance. To enable the diction of the choir to be overdone and to make sure that they were absolutely "with the stick." I learned what individual orchestra parts looked like and the various bowing articulations.

All of this time, I continued to oversee a growing program of graded choirs and handbells, including a good bit of private vocal instruction with high school students. It was in Norman that I began a series of Meet-The-Composer weekends, bringing outstanding church musicians to the church. We were fortunate to have Alice Parker as one of those and subsequently premiered one of her operas: *The Family Reunion.* We also were privileged to perform another of her operas, *Martyrs' Mirror.*

After thirteen years in Norman, I moved to the First United Methodist Church of Dallas, Texas. Ten years of music making with wonderful people and the opportunity to conduct some of the best

INTRODUCTION: IN THE BEGINNING WAS THE WORD

players of the Dallas Symphony. A most memorable performance was that of Haydn's *Creation* where all of the first desk players of the orchestra participated. A high moment, indeed.

In Norman I had started work on the DMA in Choral Conducting and finished the document required during the Dallas years. "The Church Operas of Alice Parker" was the topic and, because of my association with Ms. Parker, I had access to her insights and wisdom. Our next move was to Pulaski Heights United Methodist Church in Little Rock, Arkansas, with yet another wonderful program of graded choirs. In Arkansas, I formed the first Symphony Chorus and, for one season, was interim Conductor of the Symphony itself. Additionally, I was Artistic Conductor of the Arkansas Chamber Singers, an auditioned group with high standards and an excellent performance history.

The next eighteen years were spent with undergraduate students at Houston Baptist University. Some, but not all, majored in music and I continued to pursue the same goals of musical excellence. Is it easier on the collegiate level? It is certainly different. Easier? No. Developing an excellent choral ensemble is, in my judgment, a most difficult task, requiring continual pursuit (there's that word again) of excellence on a daily basis. Bev Henson, one of my teachers, often remarked: "Who wouldn't want the good choir? However, most of us have to develop one."

After retiring from HBU, I was called to teach conducting at St. Thomas University in Houston, Texas, where I continue to work with graduate students to improve their conducting skills.

Finally, I have come to believe that this pursuit of musical excellence must involve the responsible action and reaction of the music makers. To uphold the highest standards of our art and craft without honoring those who sing and play, is a huge mistake. The atmosphere should always be collaborative with clear responsibility placed on everyone in the room. Dr. Ann Jones remarked once: "You are through with your rehearsal – you are sweating profusely – and your singers wonder what that was all about." In other words, you did much more than your part.

INTRODUCTION: IN THE BEGINNING WAS THE WORD

Do singers and players vote? Subtly, they do, of course. This collaboration of which I speak is not about voting. It is not about the popularity of the conductor. It is about the essence of working for excellence, bringing to bear what everyone in the room knows and for which everyone feels individual responsibility. Robert Shaw was once asked: "What is the first thing you do when you conduct?" His response: "I attempt to contact all of the musical intelligence in the room." I do not believe worthwhile music is ever made in an atmosphere of fear or intimidation. We allow the process to unfold. We are well-prepared to lead in the process. But, we expect the responsibility from the music makers to listen, learn, mark, and be part of the culminating musical experience. This is not weakness, but real strength. Honoring both the product AND the producers, both the music AND the music makers gives satisfaction to all.

1

An Approach to Music and the Purpose of Analysis

I love language and I love words. Had I not gone into composition, I might have liked to try to be a writer. And I don't think that's unusual. Most artists who wind up doing one thing – painting or writing or composing – probably feel that if they had not gone that route they could have gone the other; because they are all modes of expression, of saying something you feel. In my case, I think because I like good literature, setting it to music is a natural thing for me to do. -- (Dominick Argento, *Choral Journal,* June 2007, Vol. 47, No. 12, p. 29)

Somewhere in the course of our study of music we must come to grips with our added dimension of vocal/choral music. Of course, this added dimension is language. We are all forced to face the reality of "technique." The words are there. They stand squarely between us and the music, and we have to get through with as much vocal tone, understanding and finesse as possible. This lifetime study now must involve the contemplation of text as poetry, as holy writ, philosophical aesthetics, drama or sometimes just the babble of sound for sound's sake. -- (Bev Henson, unpublished notes)

Question posed: How is composing for voice different as opposed to composing for instruments?

The huge difference is words. Words are not something you put underneath musical line, like sprinkling seasoning. The whole conception has to begin with words. Music has to grow out of the words or they don't quite fit. -- (Alice Parker, *The Voice of Chorus America,* Spring 2000, p. 5)

The subtleties of language are negated when equal weight is given to every syllable. We should always look for the music in the words and expect singers to be so aware that they never "accent the un-accent-able." Then we shall all sing: "Free at last...free at last...thank God the music is free at last." -- (John Yarrington)

Sometimes all of our efforts to look at the minutia of details leave us with little information about the whole. The study of little facets must be tempered by an understanding of the entire object. We must look at the genesis of ideas. Where did material come from and where does it go? -- (Peter Boonshaft, *Teaching Music with Passion*)

Musicians strive to perform beyond the notes, to go underneath what is simply known, all the while recognizing that knowledge is never simple. This is the spiritual part of both music and being a musician: the need to go deeper into the art. No artist actually strives for perfection; we just strive to be better. -- (Patrick Summers, *The Spirit of this Place*)

In a very intense workshop for conductors, a participant rehearsing a piece by Mozart with much change of tempo and a large, vibrato filled sound, was asked: "Why are you doing it in this way?" The response was: "Because I feel it this way." The workshop leader, with edge in his voice, said: "We don't care how YOU feel it . . . how does Mozart feel it?"

Students in conducting class at HBU knew that when I stopped someone who was conducting all over the map and asked, "Why are you doing this like that?" If the answer was: "I feel it this way," the entire class emitted a low whistle which meant: "Here comes the lecture again!"

As stated earlier, "In the beginning was the word . . . the music was in that word." I would say the three "T's of choice" are, text, text, text. Before making any decisions about interpretation, one must make an appropriate choice. Following that is the tedious, arduous process of score study to reveal, not how "I feel it," but what are the essential elements of the music, and what are the questions to ask of the piece to form one's interpretation and inform creative rehearsal.

As I review new publications, I am amazed at the banal expressions of text set to uninteresting music. Without a substantial text, I seldom look further. I desire something to put before my singers that will last, will inspire, will create wonder and excitement. Subsequently the return is a rehearsal that always presents the challenge of rising to the highest expression of the choral art. A worthy text inspires grand, eloquent, subtle musical expression in which music is never laid on top but, rather, is a logical outgrowth of the music that is already in the words.

INDICTMENT OF THE CURRENT SCENE:

I often hear excellent choirs (church/school/community) and wonder about the very personal interpretation. If the selection is from the standard repertoire, there is much performance practice information and many fine recordings which serve as guide to "how the music goes." We also know that history texts make distinctions as to major style periods: Baroque, 1600 to 1750. But we also know that there is significant overlap so that a careful look is helpful in deciding on interpretation.

I believe there is a tendency to develop a "sound" which is used regardless of the work performed. Should there be a difference in sound between a Renaissance motet, a Bach cantata, a Schubert mass or a Brahms motet? How is that "sound" determined? I continue to hear performances where the almighty sound with exquisite tuning, balance, blend, tall vowels (often distorted toward "AH") becomes more important than considerations of appropriate sound, articulated with nuance as it relates to a particular style. In plainer language: many a fine choir singing at various concerts has everything in place and gives an excellent performance. Often, the conductor micro-manages every detail – over-conducts, and the singers are obviously not charged with their part of the music making. Ensemble is about everyone on stage! When we rejoice in sound for sound's-sake, distort vowels, over articulate consonants and take the liberty of a very personal interpretation (I feel it this way), the music suffers. Whatever the choice, music should be allowed to speak in its most hospitable environment. Differences in interpretation – bravo! Differences based on personal taste – boo! There is always the fear of coloring outside the lines, also, and many a performance plays it safe. I do not recommend "safe" – I do recommend thoughtful study.

FROM WHENCE DOES INTERPRETATION COME:

Looking in all the RIGHT places. As a conductor you are also your own audience. Listen to what happens within. The people sitting there must not keep the music from coming into existence. In your closed eye have the soul of other people. As a conductor you are alone. We are born alone and die alone, and are alone whenever great things happen. This makes us brothers. Courage is the basis for doing wonderful things in life, to see mistakes and go back once again, coming closer to the truth. -- (Julius Herford, unpublished notes)

I make no apology for the following ideas about studying a piece or a movement from a larger work. I also do not claim everything said as "mine own." Obviously one can tell that I have been greatly influenced by some fine teachers, often quoted here. We must begin with text and, from the beginning introduction, bring all the musicality we can bear to the project. To gain "correct" pitches and even rhythms, but not have any idea where these pitches and rhythms go – how many go together – WHERE they go – and not allow the beauty of the words to influence is folly. What doth it profit a conductor to have correctness but lose all else in the process. -- (First John)

I asked my classes: "Do you love to go to the ballet?" Most do. Next question: "Have you ever been to a ballet studio rehearsal?" No attractive costumes – no lovely orchestral music – leggings, sweat pants, an upright piano, and sweat-sweat-sweat! My students want the "after" part – lovely costumes and orchestral music, but wish to forego the "before" part – the sweat! 'Twas ever thus.

WE ARE NOT MUSICAL WHEN:

1. We attach equal weight to every syllable.
2. Ignore grouping and direction.
3. Elevate "the", "of," "and" to world-class status.
4. Do not allow the music to breathe.
5. We conductors do not breathe rhythmically with all of the color and expression we can muster and we SHOW that in our conducting preparation.
6. "Accenting the un-accent-able" never allows the music to take flight.

Instead of reading the music for the first time, it is so easy to fall into the habit of turning on the phonograph player. This prevents us from contacting music directly without the mediation of an interpreter. Feeling helpless, again and again, we must confront the music silently with our mind and ears. We must expose ourselves to this situation, so that we may become readers. A musician is not entitled to listen to a recording until he has an idea of his own. It is shameful to only copy what another conductor does. -- (Julius Herford, unpublished notes)

As a conductor/teacher, I must not succumb to the "if-you-would-just-teach-us-the-correct-pitches-and-rhythms-we-will-put-the-music-in-later." Folly! Volunteer singers especially want security. Going over and over a particular part with pitches "pounded" out on the piano is not, however, the way to a musical performance. No one really listens to pitches pounded anyway.

We should always play those PITCHES softer TO inspire listening. We must ask for: 1. grouping and direction, 2. absolutely wonderful pitch, c. beautiful, well-formed vowels, and d. consonants articulated for the sake of textual nuance - not athletic event.

There must come a moment when one sensed the entity of a work, but does not yet know the details of the work. There must be avoided the moment when the details are known but the sense of entity is lost.
-- (Julius Herford, unpublished notes)

WHAT, THEN, MAKES FOR AN INSPIRED PERFORMANCE?

1. Trusting the music
2. Trusting the music makers – involving them – teaching and training them to love the poetry they are singing - to allow the words to speak through the music – to breathe – to enjoy – not to hurry– to listen to each other.
3. Making destination a priority: grouping, that is, how far does this parcel of text want to go – are there two-note slurs, because no two notes can ever be the same – the first always has more duration than the second. Is forward motion (not speed) evident?
4. How about basic rules of articulation: Does 3 move to 1? Does 4 move to 1? Does 6 move to 1? Do we preserve the text by lifting (not breathing) and allowing the music, thus, to breathe? Do we allow consonant articulation to fulfill a musical purpose or do we make consonants painfully obvious, calling attention, not to the music, but to the "f", 'k" etc.
5. Do we make marking a cardinal principle? Circling important words or syllables – marking lifts as well as breath – showing with a downward arrow destination places (like a map) - making sense out of the texture which is almost never SATB but some form

thereof – do we look for duets and trios – whom is singing with whom? Or, are we content to have the correct notes in place with distorted vowels and all attention to tuning? (Prejudice showing)

OUR CHOICE:

1. Appropriate for the group? Essential text? Otherwise, why?
2. Challenge: Bach *Motet 1* (Texas All State Choir, 2015) suitable for high school voices? *"Friede auf Erden"* – suitable for high school voices? The question is not whether or not these outstanding students in many major high schools CAN sing this material, but should they? Aren't we in the business, in any age, to insure that our choice represents growth for our singers?
3. Do we, as conductors, study the music carefully so that we can teach efficiently and musically?
4. Do we, as conductors, use gesture to reinforce our teaching? More often than not, I see too much movement – music over-conducted; gestures which call attention to the conductor and not to the music.

Gestures must be appropriate and should serve not only to remind us of all of the above, but to allow a truly inspired performance. I tell my students to stand still and let the music come to them. If they want it louder they can increase their gesture, or softer (without bending over). Any beat may be elongated to show a specific articulation. If we have done our score study, made a good choice, trust the music AND the music makers, then we should be able to make music without looking like the guy in the circus keeping the plates spinning. (Prejudice)

Here is what I believe: We are servants of the music, not masters. When we intrude with unfounded ideas of interpretation, based on personal taste, rather than study, especially study of performance practices, we do a disservice to the music. The music WILL speak if we allow it. This is NOT about voting or about seeking group approval. It IS about responsibility to the composer's intentions! There, I feel so much better.

Three examples:
1. "Sure on this Shining Night" (in a setting by Morten Lauridsen)
2. "Four Longfellow Settings" (four songs, set by Daniel Gawthrop)
3. "You are the Music" (in a setting by Dan Forrest)

Morten Lauridsen, Daniel Gawthrop and Dan Forrest all have had week-long residencies at HBU, an invaluable experience for our students. Lauridsen reads poetry every day to his classes at USC – a practice I began at HBU. Gawthrop believes strongly that "the music is in the words" as evidenced by his unique settings of the Longfellow songs. Dan Forrest, a wonderful pianist and theorist, always allows the words to speak through his music. All three always allow the music to be the handmaiden of the text. No words are ever forced into their settings. When one reads the poetry, which is always the way I start, one can move immediately to the musical settings.

"Sure On This Shining Night"–Morten Lauridsen Peer Music (Distributed by Hal Leonard)
A plan for study:

1. Background: American poet, novelist, journalist, film critic, and social activist James Agee (1909-1955) . . . wrote the poem used for the song. The poem appears in a book of Agee's poetry published in 1934 with the title *Permit me Voyage*. The poems are linked by American subject matter and are secular in nature. The poetry is aurally rather than visually descriptive; the words are chosen more for their sound than their meaning. Alliteration plays an important role, thus the repetition of "sh" (sure, shining, shadows) – all is healed, all is health, high summer holds the earth.

IN PURSUIT OF MUSICAL EXCELLENCE

Hearts all whole, gives an impression of peacefulness and gentleness. -- (John Hortman, 23 February, 2000. *Conductor's Analysis*)

2. Conductor study: Speak text aloud, listening for the rhythm of the words, not the setting. Be aware of the reiterated sounds of "sh", "h" etc. Love them – linger over them.

   a. Think SURE (long) on this SHIN-ning (LONG, short), NIGHT (LONG) of STAR-made (LONG-short) SHAD-ows (LONG-short) ROUND (LONG). As in chant, pause for the most important syllables –this is about duration not accentuation.

   b. Sing the opening melody on a neutral syllable. Where do the notes want to go? How many go together? This wonderful melody is part and parcel of the text – nothing more or less. There is a suppleness and a sense of direction that becomes a nurtured sound – a listening sound. I love the first two measure phrases, with "poco rit" after the word "ground" and and BEFORE the upbeat (short-short) "on this" followed by a wonderful decorative melissma on the word "shining." Again, *"poco rit"* after "night" and before the shimmering long note on "shining". And the wonderful idea about a downbeat breath to set off "night." To take time at the *"poco rit"* and to allow the music to breathe is imperative.

   c. Play the accompaniment alone – what is its function, difficulty? Does it provide foundational rhythm out of which the song emerges. Play the accompaniment and sing the melody on a neutral syllable. Use words to describe the mood: "peaceful, gentle."

   d. Tempo – "Flowing, *tempo rubato*, half note about 72. Check with your metronome or tempo watch. How fast does this go to allow the text/melody to sound.

   e. Finally, what kind of song are you? This is a Broadway ballad, pure and simple.

"Four Longfellow Settings" – Daniel Gawthrop,
Dunston House (Subito Press)
1. Snowflakes 2. Aftermath 3. My Cathedral 4. Night

I am reminded of the question one of my students asked me after we sang these pieces in St. Louis at the Southwest ACDA convention. "Can we do some more of this?" asked the student. "Gawthrop?," I asked. "No, Longfellow." (He grew to love this incredible poetry largely because Dan Gawthrop set it so beautifully.)

1. Background: All Longfellow poetry is public domain and can be found in numerous collections of his poetry.
2. Conductor study: These settings are for four part chorus, a cappella. I cannot begin to describe the luxurious textual images fashioned by Longfellow and lovingly given wings by Gawthrop.

"You Are the Music" - Dan Forrest, Hinshaw Music HMC 2171

1. Background: The text comes from "Listening" by Amy Lowell from *A Dome of Many-Coloured Glass*.
2. Conductor Study: The setting is for SSAATB chorus, Solo Soprano with piano and Horn in F.

What then to say about "looking for interpretation?" Search score study, armed with all that we know and have heard – bring into play theoretical and structural understandings, melodic construction, a "sound" which allows the music to live in its most habitable environment where nothing is forced. Start with text, speaking lovingly with enormous listening. Take time. Don't hurry. Linger – love – understand. Then communicate this in the very beginning to everyone in the room. Engage "them." Help "them" understand their role in all of this. If you are a micro-manager, I fear it is because you do not trust the music makers nor do you really trust the music. It will tell you where to go and what it wants to do. My friend, Dan Ross, who taught oboe at Arkansas State in Jonesboro, Arkansas, said to me once in an orchestral rehearsal: "I love to play for you because the music talks to you."

Just as a recipe, even in Julia Child's hands, can't solve every cooking problem or guarantee success, so a page of music is only a set of instructions to the singer. Approaching it with love and understanding is the first requirement. Interpreting it with eyes, ears and mouth open is the second. And the third? Take them both with a large grain of salt: trust your senses! Enjoy! -- (*Melodious Accord* – June, 1996)

I find that I cannot, or will not, teach music to which I am not committed, in whose worth I fully believe and about which I am passionate. One of my former students, texted me the other day with this message: "Your heart for music speaks volumes to me." I do not think this possible unless I choose well the music to be sung, and love and believe in the singers, individually and collectively. I know I am not alone in this. To stand in front of singers, asking for their very best, one needs a powerful vehicle. Time is too precious and singers too valuable to deal with sub-par expressions.

When I have made my choice, I must then diligently study and analyze that choice. Fifty years of rehearsing church choirs once a week has forced me to make the best use of the available time. Diligent study, like detective work in some ways, opens possibilities for creative teaching which is what rehearsing is all about. At HBU, I had the luxury of four and one/half hours of rehearsal a week with essentially the same group of singers. At First Presbyterian Church, the Chancel Choir rehearses for two hours, once a week. In both, excellence is sought at every turn. The music and the music makers are equally important in the equation.

I love the process of score study and marking. Though time-consuming, when I ask of a piece the appropriate questions, I begin to form an interpretation with ideas for creative rehearsing leading to an inspired performance. I never discount intuition in this process, but always try to be disciplined in my study as an aid to that intuition.

Generally, for me this means:

1. The Big Picture
   a. Text
   b. Form and Structure
   c. Key Centers
   d, Melody, text, rhythm
   e. Setting, voicing, instrumentation
2. Speaking text – circling important (weighted syllables) listening to how the words feel in the mouth - looking for destination places (phrase lengths) so that we do not fall into speaking-ev-er-y syl-la-ble the same. When we attach equal weight to every syllable, we can never let the poetry live.
3. Singing each line – marking where I had problems – marking breathing places – How can one possibly be good in "error detection" if one cannot sing each part? Sometimes in rehearsal I hear: "Altos . . . did you get that?" What? Do they vote? I think not!
4. Listening to several recordings, especially of a major work.
5. Marking: solid lines for structure, identifying key centers, harmonic changes, dynamics, tempo indications, other markings.
6. Bracketing vocal or instrumental entrances, mixed meter situations, and using arrows to indicate direction of gesture.
7. "Dry Conducting." Not to be confused with "dry" or "dull" performance. I spend much time conducting silently (always in the same posture and position I use when conducting). If orchestra is involved, I deliberately make sure I am cuing where the instruments sit. This may seem like an unnecessary step, but often, in school or church, physical limitations mean that an orchestra of some size cannot always be seated in a usual formation. To give a good cue to the right side of the orchestra for the timpani entrance, only to remember that the timpani are actually on the LEFT, is considerably damaging to one's conducting reputation and credibility.

I encourage my students to write about the music they have been assigned to conduct. One said recently: "Dr. Y, I don't work very well from an outline." I responded: "I know." The time it takes to outline what one is going to say, and the discipline to be precise in description, is another way to deepen one's understanding of the piece. Writing about music is, I find, very difficult. Students today exist in a texting culture where abbreviations are prevalent. They find it difficult to express themselves in complete sentences. At HBU I had a category of "huh" and also gave a prize for the longest run-on sentence.

Some examples:
"One is true in saying that chant does not have a steady beat, but the time signature is the placement of the weighted syllables in the text." (Huh)
"Opposite of Gregorian Chant these pieces obtain a precise meter which remains consistent throughout yet pulled through interpretation and musicality." (Huh)
"Where the text receives stress and the pace of the chant is connected and must be shown in one conducting gesture." (Huh)
"Melismatic freedoms are vital to a chant, and any interpretation must be subconscious." (I have seen some of those subconscious interpretations.)
The prize winner is, however:
In conducting a "retard" (sic), one must slow down to conduct a "retard' (sic). The correct word is of course, "*ritard*." Said the student: "I put this in spell-check."

I could go on, but I doubt the reader can take much more. On the other hand, the beginning of this conductor's analysis written by former student, Josh Hortman, gives one hope:
"Such was the vocal talent of contemporary American composer, Samuel Barber that he considered becoming a professional singer as a young man. Although he never pursued such a career, his intimate

knowledge of the voice and a love for poetry would serve Barber later on in life as a composer of songs for voice and piano." I passed the complete essay out at the beginning of class every year as an example of what constituted the type of paper expected. I knew from the first two sentences that I could expect more of the same. What a relief? ("Retard," indeed.)

LISTENING SUGGESTIONS

I have seen Alice Parker take a piece of music, hold it up to her ear, and remark: "I don't hear any music." The recordings by Robert Shaw have formed my approach to music making my entire career. I have been fortunate to study with Alice Parker and to have had the opportunity to sing with Mr. Shaw in those Carnegie Hall weeks, culminating in a concert with orchestra.

The most important qualities in these recordings are:
1. Beauty of sound
2. Range of dynamics
3. Shaping of text
4. Allowing the music to breathe

In my work with choirs in church and college, I have made the text a preference. The initial reading of the text is crucial. It allows time to shape words, to understand how many words go together to make a phrase, and how important consonant articulation is to the process. One can, however, go around the hall sounding consonants like, "k", "p" "t", but, unless there is true understanding OF those words, that process is useless. Often, the entire text is published which is so helpful. Many choirs sing beautifully in tune, with a great sound, exceptional tuning, and musicality, but I hear text mangled, especially second syllables of words. I never hear enough space for breath as well. When the notation is slavishly followed, musicality suffers. This is not license for allowing personal interpretation without study to understand the composer's intentions.

I suggest the following for listening and study:

1. *Appear and inspire* – Robert Shaw Festival Singers TELARC CD 80408
2. Music of Argento, Badings, Britten, Debussy, Poulenc and Ravel
3. *Saints Bound for Heaven* - The Musicians of Melodious Accord MA 1004
4. Arrangements of folk hymns, spirituals, and original works.
5. *Then Sings My Soul* - The Mormon Tabernacle Choir and Orchestra - (I believe this choir to be the best example of allowing the text to live in its most habitable surroundings.)

JOHN YARRINGTON

READER REFLECTIONS

2

The Interpretation Myth

Analysis can help us understand the score well enough that we are not swimmers driven by a sea of emotions. Analysis lays bare the skeleton but the bones should not show through in performance. We will study the technique of composition, that the spirituality of the composer may reveal itself to us. It is a false tradition to internalize something without understanding its purpose. Our love of Beethoven must urge us to find his essence of thought. -- (Julius Herford, unpublished lecture notes)

Our main goals as conductors should be to reveal the composer's thought as expressed in his personal musical vocabulary; to unveil his work of art in its proper proportions and structure, and to act as lightning rods for his emotion. To accomplish these things, we must try to approach the composer's mind as closely as possible. This necessarily includes at least some understanding of the text and some understanding of the composers' musical reaction to the text. -- (Bev Henson, unpublished class notes)

Musicians today know that addressing the issue of historical performance practices—the who, what, why, where, and how which framed performance at the time of composition – is fundamental to understand the music itself. The presumption that the notes on the page, of and by themselves, comprise a perfect system whereby we can conclude centuries later we are performing what the composer had in mind, is clearly an insufficient premise. -- (Melinda O'Neal in "Coming to Terms with Historical Performance Practices" in *Up Front*, Guy Webb, editor)

Vaughan Williams once compared a page of music to a railway timetable. The page, he says, tells us no more about the living experience of the music than the timetable tells us about the sights to be enjoyed during the journey. -- (Peter LeHuray, *Authenticity in Performance*)

Composing is a terribly abstract art form. Yet composers will tell you a piece well composed, which communicates deeply, is their reason for being, their reason for life. That journey of seeking a way in which to communicate through sound, pitch, time and duration is their *raison d'etre*. The results of the journey, which we call a piece of music, are fragile at best and communicative at their deepest. If we are very fortunate and work very hard, that ordering of sound in time and space has meaning across the ages, across the cultures, and across time. -- (Libby Larsen in *Pan Pipes*, Spring, 2001)

It must be admitted that in the period around 1900, many artists overdid themselves in exhibiting the power of the emotion they were capable of feeling; artists who believed themselves to be more important than the work – or at least than the composer. -- (Arnold Schoenberg, from *Style and Idea*)

For me, the durations on the page are as close as I can get to duplicating for the eye, what I am speaking/singing aloud when I read the text well. I am not squeezing the syllables into the note heads; I am allowing the pitch to clothe the vibrant reading with its own magic. And how about those pitches. Are high notes the same as low, in their production and sound? Should a forte high "f" in the soprano sound as loud as a forte low "d"? What can the page do? It can transmit the baldest information about text, pitches, rhythms and performance values across time and space. -- (Alice Parker, *Melodious Accord*, June 1996)

In a fall concert at HBU, the following pieces were sung:
a. "Holy God, We Praise Thy Name" – John Ferguson GIA G-3167
b. "Come Thou Almighty King" – setting by Michael Burkhardt MorningStar MSM-60-9029
c. "*Os Justi*" – Anton Bruckner Edition Peters Peters 6315
d. "*Sanctus in d minor*" -- J.S. Bach Alliance AMP 0361
e. "*O Sacrum Convivium*"-- Dan Locklair Subito Music 492-0006
f. "Wake Every Breath" – William Billings public domain
g. "*Ecco Mormorar L'Onde*" – Claudio Monteverdi Oxford University Press OCCO15
h. "*Intende voce oratione*" – Franz Schubert Arista Music Company
i. *Te Deum* – John Rutter

The program began with bells ringing from all four corners of the chapel with the choir processing, surrounding the audience with sound. The final piece was a seven minute setting of the *Te Deum* for choir, organ and brass. In between, was music representing various style periods. This was our opening concert for the fall season which involved an advanced choir, *Schola Cantorum*, and a second choir, University Singers. For several of the pieces, both groups sang together. The plan in choosing this literature was to establish the basics of ensemble: tuning, vowels, tone color, appropriate articulation, breath energy, marking, while establishing individual responsibility for attention to all of the above. I believe, as I have stated earlier, that one must honor both the music and the music makers. This is not about voting. It is about each person's responsibility to the ensemble which also includes attendance, energy, enthusiasm, and just plain hard work. Both groups had some challenge. Each sang in at least one other language. We started the concert, after the processional, with a hymn anthem which gave everyone, choir and audience alike, the opportunity to sing. Alice Parker has often remarked: "No choral concert is complete until everyone sings."

HBU is a small, liberal arts school, with only undergraduates in music. I believe that for many, conductors, programming very difficult music may have more to do with the image of the conductor, than with the educational experience for both chorus and audience. To consider what forces one has and plan accordingly is important. To challenge with literature is crucial. On the other hand, music a bit more accessible, allows ensemble development which grows and matures as the year progresses. I also believe that taking the audience into consideration without catering is important. If we do not take care of our audiences by providing a listening foothold, we shall surely lose them. We will be left with parents, grandparents, and the casual person off the street. Symphony Orchestras, opera companies and smaller, professional musical groups all contend with this reality. So should we.

In the spring of that year, we sang choruses from Haydn's *Creation* and the Beethoven's *Mass in C*, with professional orchestra. Closing out the year was a presentation of the opera, *Family Reunion*, by Alice Parker. We received an NEA grant for this and Ms. Parker conducted.

I believe that a program of individual works should be interesting to the audience. We should not ignore the listeners in our choices. Differing styles, languages, a cappella works, accompanied works, all contribute to both audience appeal and choir development.

We cannot escape our obligation to read about style and performance practice, listen to recordings, speak to colleagues, attend concerts, to sharpen our ability to allow the music to live through an informed interpretation. How many times have we heard concerts with fabulous intonation, beautiful vowels, etc., but with little or no change in sound or color. How different is the sound needed for Bruckner, Locklair, Monteverdi, Rutter or an arrangement of a spiritual? If we are diligent in our study and remember what we learned in school, and listen and learn from others, I believe the sounds have to have variety because of the inherent style demands. Were I to make a checklist of the important qualities of style inherent in each of the aforementioned pieces, it would look like this:

a. "Holy God": based on chant/single line melody, not non-vibrato, but with careful attention to pitch and beauty of vowel. This is music in which the sound should not call attention to itself. Its use was in worship and the singing was often in very live acoustical settings. It is not, however, anemic or non-energetic. The rhythm of chant is, after all, the rhythm of the words and this subtlety carries over into all of our work with text. The listening quotient is enormously important.

b. "Come Thou Almighty King" (hymn anthem): This is a classical hymn –think string quartet – it is notated in three but moves in a graceful one to a bar. I learned at HBU that many of our students (remember that not all of these singers are music majors) did not grow up singing hymns like "Come Thou Almighty King." I programmed a hymn arrangement to begin and end the program as a way to expand the singers' repertoire of hymns and also to involve the audience in singing. I also had to teach the hymn itself, before teaching the arrangement.

c. "*Os Justi*" (Bruckner): Fuller sound (much different sound from that of "Come Thou Almighty King") employing depth and core of vowels and concentrating on tuning, especially in the divisi sections. A wider vocal range is essential and there is opportunity to use this fuller more focused sound to shape lengthy phrases with, as Mr. Shaw used to say, "beginning, middling, and ending." Developing awareness for one's own part in the whole is also a goal. Important vocal lines must be allowed to sing. This is different from asking one section to sing louder. We can teach much about structure from this experience.

d. "*Sanctus in d minor*": early Baroque, light texture with a sound reference of flute or recorder. Awareness of a dancing quality and the importance of letting short notes move toward the next longer note. Again, Mr. Shaw used to say: "The short notes are looking for a place to sit down." Tone quality here uses the above-mentioned sound reference and much can be accomplished by singing (dancing) on a neutral syllable, listening more than singing.

e. "*O Sacrum, con Vivium*": The piece is enhanced by a rich, resonant organ accompaniment. Rhythm of the music is again, the rhythm of the words, here notated, and the aim is to allow the notation to serve the music and not the other way 'round. Locklair set the text beautifully, using the organ as a tonal fabric.

f. "Wake Every Breath" (Billings): Early American canon in six parts. Square style with sturdy downbeat, notated in three but moves in one. There is the physical sense of lifting up one's foot and planting it down at the beginning of every bar, like a square dance.

g. "*Ecco Mormorar*" (Monteverdi): Text shape is crucial. Homophonic sections are balanced by some of the most interesting chromatic and harmonic passages imaginable. The listening quotient is essential so that not only do chords tune, but awareness is fostered. There is seldom, in any music, a full four-part SATB. In this work, there are variations, solos, duets, trios.

h. "*Intende voci orationis meae*" (Schubert): An offertory setting for tenor solo, chorus and orchestra or organ. I chose this, frankly, to give one of our senior tenors a chance in the spotlight. It is luxurious, tuneful music which allows one's intuition about phrase shape and length full reign. There are some fugal places, often the chorus echoes what the soloist has just sung. Accompaniment is based on string arpeggiation figures which work on the organ. This is an accessible piece for the audience.

i. *Te Deum* (Rutter): A well-crafted, seven minute exposition of a profound, historical text which was important for my students to know. As in the case of the hymn tunes, the Rutter is full of brilliant music for brass, organ and timpani, text well set, and a breathtaking final hymn tune with an RKO ending.

The above are style snapshots. The reader with much experience may think, "too brief" or pedestrian, but the intent is to get the less-experienced conductors among us to think, to question, to listen, to score study, and to make informed performance decisions. The hymn tune which closes the *Te Deum* written by John Rutter is a magnificent, stirring melody which soars.

Not to belabor the point, but each of these pieces has a history and some established performance practice which allows for creative teaching and rehearsing and for a performance full of the individual life represented. Would all of us agree about appropriate sound or performance practice? Not only would we not agree, but *vive le difference*. When I listen to more than one recording of the same work, I am constantly enlivened and return to score study enriched. My job is not to copy what someone else has done, but to make of rehearsal and performance an exciting, energetic, energy-filled performance with all the understanding I can muster. I trust my intuition, as I have said earlier, but only if it is informed by careful study.

Sally Herman in her book, *In Search for Musical Excellence*, gives Rules of Articulation which I find most valuable:

a. Never accent the last note of a phrase or the last syllable of a word.
b. All phrases begin where the previous one left off.
c. No two consecutive notes or phrases should be alike.
d. Place "lifts" or "accents" on weak beats or off beats.
e. When a dotted note is followed by a note of shorter value, place the accent on the short note: (1) Put a slight space between the dotted note and the short note, and, (2) Put a slight crescendo on the dotted note.
f. When the basses have a descending octave leap, put an accent on the second note and pull into the next note, especially at cadence points. Put a slight space between the two notes of the octave leap.

It is easy to fall into the trap of establishing what we want for a particular phrase and then making all phrases that are of the like rhythmic and melodic shape the same. Each phrase can be thought of as forming circles that begin at one dynamic level and make changes according to the arsis and thesis of the line. A new circle begins but must be connected to the first circle . . . the sizes of the circles vary as we expand dynamic levels within the phrase. The text will always help us make decisions as to how we want to change like phrases if it differs when the notes and rests do not. -- (Sally Herman, *In Search of Musical Excellence*)

In the final analysis, do I wish to hear heart-felt singing, out of tune, with garbled consonants, sloppy articulation – well-intentioned, but not well sung? None of us wants this. But equally do I not want to hear a choir drilled to perfection, with a singular tone quality regardless of style – a choir whose established sound never changes. For me, this represents "dull" on steroids and "dull" is a four-letter word in my book.

As we listen to a choir, do we envy what we are hearing? I believe this is to be expected. But there is rejoicing when we hear an excellent group, even if we do not agree with the sound or interpretation. We should be glad about difference expressed in this way and be willing to examine some of our own ideas in the light of new ideas and sounds. Safety, on the other hand, should not be the primary goal. We should always care more about our obligation to present music in an interpretation honed by careful score study while taking into account the ability of the performers we have – not the ones we WISH we had. Roger McMurrin, when serving at Highland Park Presbyterian Church in Dallas, once remarked: "I believe we often program for our colleagues."

In other words, we plan and prepare works often beyond the ability of those we conduct. "When are you going to perform the Britten *War Requiem* at HBU?" I was asked. "Never," was the answer. Not because I am not capable of teaching or conducting it, but because in a small, undergraduate music school, we cannot and should not do this. We must be very aware of the vocal development of our singers, especially young ones. Because an accomplished high school choir can sing the Schoenberg *"Friede Auf Erde"* doesn't mean that they should or that it is in their best interest. Is it great music? Oh, my yes! Will it ever be performed? Yes, it will. Does my group have the horse-power to do the music justice? Ah, there's the question. (There is a wonderful article in the *Choral Journal*, April 2012, Vol. 52, No. 9 called "On The Voice", Sharon Hansen, Editor. Sub-heading: The Top Ten Complaints from Both Sides of the Aisle. I recommend this highly.)

JOHN YARRINGTON

READER REFLECTIONS

3

Vocal Athletes

A recent survey disclosed that there are 15,000,000 choral singers in the world. A conservative estimate that at least 95% do not study voice with a private voice teacher, would indicate that 24,250,000 singers worldwide are learning all their vocal technique from their choral directors. What a heady responsibility and a grand opportunity! -- (Paul Brandvik, in *Up Front*, edited by Guy Webb, p. 149)

Snapshot #1: Beginning in C Major, the enthusiastic choral conductor begins rehearsal, using scale patterns 1 to 5, on the syllables "mah, may, mee, moh, moo." The exercise begins on C and moves upward by half steps.

Snapshot #2: Using *solfeggio* and hand signals, this director works for energy in a variety of short phrases, with the intent of solidifying pitch, and intervallic security. The beginning pitch is low and vowel sounds used are ill-formed and edgy.

Snapshot #3: Beginning in C Major, this warm-up uses scale steps 5 to 1 on "AH" and moves downward by half steps. Sometimes a different vowel is substituted.

Snapshot #4: A phrase or song is used for warmup like "My mommy munches M and M's." You know the type.

What is wrong with these pictures?

1. Never begin in C Major! This immediately engages the lower register or heavy mechanism sound of the voice – the speaking voice register, if you will. Singers already operate well in that part of the voice. We should always begin in mid-register and move up or down, with the notion of what William Vennard called the "yawn-sigh." That is, an easy, cool air breath, which lifts the palate, while releasing the jaw, to produce a sound filled with energy but not weight.

2. With the good intent of *solfeggio* and hand signals as an aid to music reading and intervallic recognition, the sounds used must be the best one can utter. To allow ill-formed vowels, with tight jaws, and edgy sound to accomplish this is nonsense. Someone said to me once in a rehearsal after hearing this travesty: "Could you fix those vowel sounds?" They should not have to be "fixed." Nothing should go on in any rehearsal that is not based on well-formed vowels, sung on the breath with released jaw. (Not "dropped jaw," by the way).

3. Obviously like #1. Beginning in a key which engages the lower register sound and proceeding DOWNWARD is folly and leads to an attempt to produce the upper register pitches with lower registration. #3 is worse than #1.

4. Some of you know I have used the warm-up beginning "Many mumbling mice..." but only after stretching, loosening up, and beginning in the key of E flat major, starting on the fifth, or B flat. I have also used the collection *Sing Legato*. (Neil A Kjos, V74A, Accompaniment Version.) Written by Ken Jennings, these are still used by the St. Olaf Choir in warming up. These offer a worthy substitute to simply vocalizing on vowel sounds. They are interesting and accomplish the purposes intended.

A common idea is that we don't have time to warm-up – it should be done outside of the rehearsal time. I believe that we must warm-up because, in the long run, it saves time. Imagine, if you will, a symphony orchestra, coming on stage, and beginning to play the first piece. What actually happens? The instrumentalists tune up, noodle around on their instruments, play difficult passages, and get ready. Then, they tune, first winds and brass, then strings. THEN they play! Notice that they TUNE up before they play. Imagine that concept! After more than fifty years of directing choirs of children, youth and adults in church situations, the tuning up is just as important as the warming up. From the first, we should ask everyone in the room to come together as an ensemble and to be responsible to each other for beautiful vowels, energetic breath and singing in tune. I mentioned earlier my first experiences with the youth choir at a former church. Sixty kids in the room – breath taken – sound emitted MOSTLY BREATH. Also, in youth or middle-school choir, some folks singing below the pitch. What to do? The whole area of changing voices is worth another chapter, but thankfully, much has now been written about this area.

When working with children or youth or adults, there is a common thread and approach to singing with beauty. It is important to understand what is age-appropriate for each group and how sound is produced from a child, a youth, or an adult. Warm-ups should always center on proper alignment, energetic but not effortful breath, released jaw and vowel sounds tall and well-shaped. While the approach is certainly different with each age group, the principles are essentially the same:

In children: developing what Helen Kemp called the "singing channel" has been the guiding principle of many of us. Our culture dotes on singing in "chest" with a microphone. Think of all of the "American Idol" types of contests. Much of that singing is in lower register or speaking voice – I have called that "pageant voice," and it is very hard to move someone to a fuller, more productive vocal development, when only about six notes are sung in "chest" and, when moving out of that, the rest of the singing sounds like whispering.

In youth: No one is really a first soprano or a second alto. Most young female singers have basically a second soprano register. We should work to develop that range both upward and downward and we should not put the better readers on alto, forcing them into that range and developing what I have called in earlier writings an "alto mentality." That is, "God did not intend me to sing any note above the fourth line in the treble clef." If our male singers are ever to have facility above middle C, we must help them by developing their upper register sound. Falsetto is a great help in this regard.

We have a tendency to think that changing voices are only in the male species, but that is also not true. Female voices also need help in this area. However, with male singers, we often equate lower notes with masculinity and allow singers to push down on their larynx in order to achieve that result. It is so important for them to understand that nothing is "broken" and that this vocal development is very usual and ordinary. I hate the term "broken." An arm is "broken," a leg is "broken," but a voice is NOT broken. We have to work individually to encourage our male singers to use all of the voice they have and to move from falsetto down into the changing or changed voice.

In adults: Our problem here, especially in volunteer church choirs, is that some of our folks have been singing the same way for many, many years. To suggest to the sopranos, for instance, that they should approach upper notes with lightness, steady breath and released jaw, is to draw that "look" which most of us recognize.

"Let me alone," is that "look" – "I have sung this way all my life and I am not about to change." The altos love to be in lower register but have trouble moving up. God forbid that they might have to sing something along with the sopranos which goes above fourth line "D" in the treble staff. The tenors – oh well – let's leave them alone. We are so grateful for them, aren't we? Then, there are the basses, most of whom are really baritones or barely-tones who love to set those jaws and bellow below the staff. Recognize anyone? They must learn to use their upper regis-

IN PURSUIT OF MUSICAL EXCELLENCE

ter sound and they CAN do this, but it is painful – for you, and FOR THEM.

What do we all want from our ensembles?

1. Beauty of sound – on the breath
2. Dynamic range – not dwelling in "mezzo-land." A real "piano" occasionally, for instance.
3. Beautifully formed vowel sounds with released jaw. As you look at your group, you see an assortment of vowel shapes. Attempting to get everyone to form the same vowel at the same time is what we all want. Getting there is the hard part.
4. Aligned bodies – many of our problems occur because we allow singers to stand without a tall body and to sit slouched. Holding music is a major culprit. A Yarrington-ism is: "Where your music is, there will your eyes be also." (First John) I have some folks in the Presbyterian Choir I direct who never look up! This means that they place their larynx in an impossible position, and are also not able to respond to the fabulous gestures coming from the podium!
5. Appropriate diction, which starts with appreciation of textual beauty and shape. As long as we accent the un-accent-able (je-SUS, shep-HERD, fa-THER, instead of JE-sus, SHEP-herd, and FA-ther), we are not musical. Attaching equal weight because of notation to words whose shape is UN-EQUAL makes for a terribly unsatisfying musical experience. In my words, "not a religious experience."

My checklist is as follows:

1. Always warm- and tune-up. Always begin with stretching and loosening up. Make listening and tuning-up a priority. Do not allow loud singing in the beginning of any rehearsal, but also,

do not allow unsupported, tight-jawed, lowered palate singing. NEVER BEGIN IN C MAJOR.
2. Vary the routine. Nothing is as dull as the same set of exercises done in the same way every time. Challenge the singers, sometimes with simple rote exercises or even clapping, much as you do with children, for instance. Use excerpts from current literature and also hymns: "Come Thou Almighty King" or "Come, Christians, Join to Sing" or "All Creatures of our God and King" emphasizing an approach which begins in the upper register. Helen Kemp used to caution: "The lower the lighter." Often our adult singers particularly, love to head for the "bottom," adding weight and pulling the pitch down as well.
3. Plan and write out what you are going to do. Five minutes of a warm-up/tune-up is an enormous amount of time when wisely used. Your voice is your best model. Sing to them what you want and then listen to see what comes back. Encourage, don't scold!
4. Always have the following categories in mind: the physical, the mental, the flexible and the dynamic.
5. I employ the T.U.B method: Start from the TOP (Vennard yawn sigh), UNHINGE THE JAW (Don't "drop" it), engage the BREATH.
6. What you do can be fun as well as productive. Above all, DON'T TALK. "They" don't really care about the actual techniques you are using. You will bore them at best or scare them off by "explaining." Use one section as a model. Ask them to sing – ask the rest of the choir to listen – sometimes, like the Christians and the Lions, we give a thumbs UP or DOWN – always in a good-natured way. Use antiphonal hymns as listening aids. Make some of what you do a game – even adults love to play, though some have lost that sense. Life has a way of doing that!
7. Make sure that range is exercised, both high and low.
8. Make sure that dynamics are experienced – try singing, using the numbers 1 to 8, adding energy to each succeeding number. In

other words, crescendo from 1 to 8. Decrescendo from 8 to 1. Have "them" listen. I don't know about your choir, but mine loves to sing "mf" and above. Even when "p" or "pp" is marked!

We all know that the way we warm-up and rehearse is the way we are going to sound. The notion that the "Holy Spirit" is going to endow us with a quality and articulation for which we have not worked is an affront. Truly, no one in the congregation or, for that matter, the audience really understands our process. They see a final result but do not see the blood, sweat and tears which precede. Our job as conductors is to allow our people to grow in their ability to be messengers and purveyors of beauty regardless of repertoire. A spiritual must have as much accurate performance practice as does a Bach chorale. Each must live in its most suitable environment with appropriate sound.

JOHN YARRINGTON

READER REFLECTIONS

4

Rehearsal Strategies

You want to arrive at the first rehearsal with a set of options, credible enough for a genuine choice rather than a dilemma and you need the ability to choose between these possibilities and take ownership of the consequences of those choices as quickly as possible. -- (Mark Wigglesworth, *The Silent Musician*)

Robert Shaw encouraged all singers to save their "vocal gold" – meaning to pace themselves. As a choral conductor, I want my singers to come to rehearsal ready to sing- physically, mentally, and vocally. I must be careful to remember that forty minutes of practicing is considered the outside limit before a voice requires at least fifteen minutes of rest. I must organize my rehearsal plans in such a way that I allow individual sections of the choir to rest their voices while doing a musical activity (tapping/clapping/snapping rhythms, sitting quietly). I must pace myself so I teach the music in a didactic manner that causes the details to stick, so that frequent repetition is not required. My rehearsal must be disciplined, but not tense. -- (Brenda Smith, in "On the Voice," *Choral Journal*, Vol. 52, No. 9)

The goal of every choral director is to produce a warm, vital and energetic choral sound that is correct for a particular composition and also pleasing to the ear. Since each singer has a different, personal concept of sound, it is the task of the conductor to unify these divergent concepts into a somewhat homogeneous realization of his own tonal concepts. -- (Sharon Hanson, *Choral Journal,* December 1999, p. 81)

Rehearsal time is like a clothes closet. No matter how much closet space we have, we want more. As well, the amount of space needed increases as the amount made available increases. -- (Peter Boonshaft, *Teaching Music with Passion*)

With more than fifty years of experience in working with volunteer singers of all ages in a church situation, I have come to value time as an essential element of success in rehearsal. When one rehearses only once a week, much has to be accomplished every time you meet. One of my ministerial friends described Sunday as the "relentless Sabbath." I often remark that only a church choir presents music each and every Sunday of the year. High School choirs, University choirs and Community Choral groups typically present several concerts a year. I will acknowledge that the repertoire for such concerts is often of more difficulty than the weekly grind of music for worship, but I tried to teach my students, to prepare as if their very lives depended on it.

Another consideration is that of working with a professional orchestra. This will be discussed in a subsequent chapter, but when you hire professional players, you have only a certain amount of time. If you do not finish rehearsing what you plan to perform in that time, as the players are putting up their instruments they will say: "Thank you, Doctor Yarrington." A polite way of saying "we are through."

In working with Robert Shaw in several of those Carnegie Hall experiences, I marveled at the organization and precision of the rehearsals. We were engaged in a major work each time, and he squeezed music out of every single minute! This came home to me in an interesting way. We were rehearsing the Beethoven *Missa Solemnis* with orchestra and were on the very last page of the work. The orchestra contractor sidled up to Mr. Shaw (while he was conducting!) and whispered: "You have 30 seconds." Shaw finished – cut everyone off - and then, to those of us

IN PURSUIT OF MUSICAL EXCELLENCE

seated in the front rows remarked: "Actually . . . I had one minute." His work all those years in radio with Fred Waring had honed his skill to the point that his inner clock was always on. Thirty seconds is an enormous amount of time, not to mention one minute! The point is that one counts the cost when rehearsing, either vocal forces or vocal and orchestral forces. By that I mean that you plan and time what you attempt to accomplish. Time is precious whether one is paid or not. Being "professional" means giving one's best the entire time. Someone asked me once, "How long do you rehearse?" I answered: "**I** rehearse for two hours." That answer was lost on the questioner but those reading know what I mean. When on the podium, you cannot doze or look around, or make comments, or just simply loaf. The energy required to successfully complete a rehearsal of any kind is enormous and focus and timing are essential. I must know what has to be accomplished THIS REHEARSAL while keeping in mind the larger picture. In church, anthems are usually balanced by a major work of some kind. In school, there is more music to learn, often in an unfamiliar language (although, I have to say that, in Texas, English is a foreign language) and it is often of considerable difficulty. I know many collegiate situations where the luxury of several weekly rehearsals is squandered to the point that when concert time rolls around, there are suddenly extra rehearsals and lots and lots of pressure.

My Rehearsal Check-list:

1. Begin with appropriate stretching, breathing, singing and tuning. A warm-up should be planned – five minutes is lots of time if one moves quickly and knows exactly what is to be accomplished. I think the attitude from the podium that this part of the rehearsal is crucial rubs off on the singers.
2. Start with something familiar.
3. Work toward the most difficult anthem or section of a major work and taper off. A rehearsal should feel like movements of a

symphony culminating in a feeling of success. Last-minute pressure when careful work was not done earlier, seldom leads to an inspired performance.

The placement of a given piece of music within a rehearsal is extremely important if direction, vigor, variety and persistence are to be successfully maintained during the learning development. Familiar works that require a minimum of rehearsal time should follow the opening warm-up in the learning exposition. As the rehearsal progresses, more complex works, newly introduced works, and ultimately the most technically complex compositions are introduced. -- (Lawrence Kaptein, *Choral Journal,* November 1987)

How is this accomplished?

1. CHOICE – a variety of styles and difficulty with honest awareness of the ability of our singers and instrumentalists.
2. STUDY - Careful score study reveals rehearsal possibilities: I always begin with text – often reading aloud musically, to hear the shapes of individual words as well as destination points and rhyme schemes. So often, because we are such "page-people," we equate the black blobs (notes – as Alice Parker calls them) with the music to be made. Ms. Parker always says that "your voice is your best model." I have observed many a professional orchestral conductor singing to the ensemble demonstrating clearly what is desired. When I demonstrate, using my voice, I bring all of the color, nuance, text articulation and beauty I can muster.

I attempt to keep everyone engaged: if two parts are singing, the other two parts are speaking text lightly, or using a neutral syllable, or count-singing. I love to find duets and trios in the music which is another way of helping everyone see their part of the score. Bev Henson used to tell the choir: "Know your part and know what you are a part of."

Many of us use count-singing, neutral syllables, whispering and various ways of solidifying the ensemble. Mr. Shaw rehearsed on a four-part chord chanting the text as yet another way to accomplish unity.

Often, I ask singers to pair up and sing to each other. One is certainly more responsible when one is audited. (Think of the IRS.) A scrambled arrangement (or "singing confused" as John Ferguson refers to it) is helpful. Asking individual sections to form a circle and sing into each other or seating the choir in a large circle makes for more careful listening. One must take care of what comes out of one's own mouth.

Sectional rehearsal works very well as long as the musical aspects are integrated. To "pound" notes without any realization about where those notes go . . . or how MANY go together . . . does not move the process forward.

There are always those who think that, if the correct pitches are learned, the music can then be added. Not so! Accompanists should always, in my view, play accurately and softly so that singers actually listen. How many times, in frustration, has a director asked an accompanist to "pound" out a part or has, actually sung loudly WITH the section as if that would actually help. When one sings with the choir, one really cannot hear what is being produced. Frustrated as we sometimes are by bad vowels, poor pitch, garbled diction, not to mention ev-er-y word-sung-the-same, our job is to keep the musical goal always foremost.

Too much talking from the podium is another waste of time. When one cuts off, one should know exactly where to go and what to "fix." "Alright, let's do that again," seldom is successful. Someone in the choir should yell: "WHAT DO YOU WANT TO BE DIFFERENT?" When we continue to say "blend, blend, blend . . ." someone should yell: "WE WILL BLEND, IF YOU WILL TELL US WHERE, WHEN AND WITH WHOM."

Tidbits from unpublished notes working with Dr. Ann Howard Jones:

*Don't get in there and make noises with them.
*Make a radical commitment to the vowel
*We have to know what we want to hear – and what color.
*Engage the music maker in the rehearsal.
*It is impossible to avoid scholarship.
*You can't avoid score preparation. Look for what the composer "wants." Music is the persistent focus of man's intelligence, aspiration and good will. It is not a luxury but a necessity.

EXPECTATION

The more I expect the ensemble to see and hear what needs to be done, the better the product. If I chose artistic texts, full of nuance and meaning and focus on the poetry and music in the words, not on the notes, the closer I am to realizing what the composer intended. Not "the way I feel it," but what my careful score study reveals.

There must come a time when one sensed the entity of a work, but does not yet know the details of the work. There must be avoided the moment when the details are known but the sense of entity is lost. -- (Julius Herford, unpublished lecture notes)

My job is to raise the awareness of the entire ensemble. If I expect tall vowels, full of beauty, crisp, effective consonants, musical awareness of word shapes, destinations, phrase shapes, I must work on these diligently, even relentlessly. Tuning is not an accident – it must have careful work. Music must be "in the bones" and that only happens when everyone participates. Mr. Shaw used to remark, "the beauty is in the details." So, for me, it is a precarious balance between looking at the whole while focusing on the smallest detail. Easier said than done!

Speaking of Mr. Shaw, in an address in Norman, Oklahoma, November 19, 1977, he said, "The understandings of the spirit are not easily come by. It takes a creative mind to respond to a creator's mind. It takes a Holy Spirit to receive the Holy Spirit. And, 'Just as I am,' is not nearly good enough."

JOHN YARRINGTON

READER REFLECTIONS

5

Understanding Articulation – the Long and Short of It

> Never accent the un-accent-able!
> Trust the music – it will tell you where it wants to go.
> Do not hurry – speed kills.
> "I feel it this way" is tantamount to musical disaster.
> (John Yarrington)

Most singers can achieve wonderfully musical results, because they don't know they can't. In other words, they are not hampered by too much "education." They respond to text, phrasing and articulation out of what I call the "Horse-Sense-Quotient." All of this on one rehearsal a week.

I was blessed with university choirs rehearsing several times a week, many were majoring in music, but, truthfully, some of the best singers were NOT majoring in music.

I was blessed with a wonderfully supportive vocal faculty which I know is not the case in many situations. On Friday mornings, the vocal majors assembled for Voice Performance Class. They sang and then were critiqued by someone other than their own teacher. I sat on vocal juries. Often, one or more vocal faculty came to rehearsal to assist in concert preparation. The atmosphere created was extremely healthy and students perceived that their teachers were all working together.

Having said that, my frustration in both in church and school, is that we live in a LONG-LONG world – that is – we attach equal weight to every note bearing a syllable instead of carefully speaking the text with love and care and appreciation and "never accenting the un-accentable." I constantly work for phrase shape, articulation (which, for me means not always breathing – sometimes "lifting") and for destination. Mr. Shaw always said that music was "pah-DAH" not "DAH-DAH." In other words, we SHOULD live in a "short-LONG" or, to be fancy, an anacrusic world because music moves forward in that way.

From a wonderful book, *Phrasing and Articulation, A contribution to a Rhetoric of Music,* by Hermann Keller:

The words "phrasing" and "articulation" have basically different meanings: "phrasing" is much like the subdivision of thought (phrases) and to set them off from one another; it has thus the same function as punctuation marks in language. "He who phrases incorrectly is like a man who does not understand the language he speaks," said Chopin to his student Mikuli. Hans von Bulow expressed it similarly: "In music, we must punctuate, phrase, separate: we must play the piano, not babble." The function of musical articulation on the other hand is the binding together or the separation of the individual notes; it leaves the intellectual content of a melody line inviolable, but it determines its expression. There is, therefore, as a rule only one possible, thoughtful phrasing; but there are several articulation possibilities.

Phrasing and articulation as attributes of the melodic line are the two areas best understood through analogy to language: A merely pure, merely correct performance is worth only as much as a spelling in sound. It belongs with the rudiments. Clear enunciation is still not understandable declamation; meaningful declamation is still not sensitive and therefore expressive eloquence. An art of performance in musical language must above all be grounded in the working together of three factors, in which each higher element depends upon the lower. -- (Herman Keller, *Phrasing and Articulation*)

In working with a conducting student this summer, I was reminded that I have a process of looking at a piece of music which I teach. Most of this will seem obvious, I am sure, to those of you with experience, but, the longer I teach conducting, the more I am aware that many of my students simply do not know how to look at a piece of music with any understanding of the basics of form, harmony, theory, text. They do not conduct well what is assigned because of a lack of study and understanding:

1. This process is not a matter of length of material. A three minute anthem takes the same sort of careful study as does a multi-movement work.
2. Choice is crucial. A worthy text well set is always the first step. Anything else is not worth the effort.
3. Begin with text. Carefully speak, listening for rise and fall of individual syllables, rhyme scheme, destination, and where you breathe. (Alice Parker memorizes the text first before setting it to music.)
4. Look at the large picture first: with a pencil, make a check where a phrase ends, where a new section begins (textually, musically) and then put solid bar lines at those places. A formal, structural picture begins to emerge.
5. Dynamics: I use only two colors – feel free to exist in a Technicolor world – Red for various shades of loud, blue for various shades of soft. Circles or boxes. Sometimes a different dynamic marking exists in only one part. More importantly, seldom should all parts sing at the same dynamic. The most important line needs to be highlighted, which means that everyone in the room is AWARE and adjusts as necessary.
6. Look for duets and trios – who sings with whom – if there is a unison passage, this is a great chance to work on ensemble, phrasing, and destination.

7. In rehearsal, one begins with all the musicality to be mustered. It is ridiculous and a time-waster to pound notes and then attempt to put the music in later. "If we pound it, they will learn it." Nonsense! As Peter Boonshaft, observes: "Why is there never enough time to do things right...but always enough time to do them over." -- (*Teaching Music with Passion*, p. 6)

8. Creativity in rehearsing. One's study enables creative teaching. If you desire to stand on the podium, you'd better be prepared BEFORE you step up there. If you are not prepared or if you are attempting to learn along with your choir, everyone knows it. You can yell: "WATCH ME." But someone should yell back: "FOR WHAT?"

9. Planning in rehearsal. There is only so much time. Every rehearsal should have a plan, beginning with a five-minute warm-up/tune-up and then a realistic assessment of how much can be accomplished. Timings at the side of each piece made in the cool light of day, keep one on track. Too much time spent on any one piece, especially in church, means that somewhere along the line our group will go into the loft unprepared. With a church choir rehearsing once a week, one has to have a "readiness timetable." The Wednesday or Thursday before a scheduled anthem is to be sung should be a time for polishing; not that last-minute, agonized, stressful, rehearsal where everyone is exhausted but still unprepared. It is a kamikaze mission at best anyway, because some missed several rehearsals along the way for this particular Sunday, but show up anyway to sing on Sunday. The Lord told them to come on. Too bad the Lord didn't tell them how important it was to be at rehearsal. Again, from the wisdom of Peter Boonshaft: ". . . it could be just a little outline. But I think we have to have something, for if we don't we are just winging it, and winging it always scares me in that it usually wastes time. Time is one thing we don't have to waste."

IN PURSUIT OF MUSICAL EXCELLENCE

READER REFLECTIONS

6

The Energy Mystique

More Results from less-effortful Conducting:
Don't be careful – work for energy – find the energy.
Nothing is as boring as accuracy. You must ask yourself as a singer:
"Would anyone want to hear what I am doing?"
You may not perform in an ordinary manner.
(Don Neuen, unpublished class notes)

Conducting is a series of preparations – every beat sets up
the next one with gestures unaffected by mannerisms of any kind.
Score preparation: Do you practice what you are going to show?
Don't get in there and make noises with them.
Engage the music maker in the rehearsal.
(Ann Jones, unpublished class notes)

Music is basic to the human condition. Our job, as conductors,
is to help people do what comes naturally: to select,
refine and polish; to organize, enable and encourage. We're not
asking anyone to perform an unnatural act!
So why do we often place ourselves in the position of
taskmaster and disciplinarian, imposing our will on
a reluctant ensemble or audience? Do we dominate our
choirs for the sake of an artistic product, or to fortify our egos?
(Joshua R. Jacobson, *Massachusetts ACDA Choral News*)

IN PURSUIT OF MUSICAL EXCELLENCE

We need to listen to our own inner voice, which is our innermost personal musical idea. At all times, we must both listen to the music within us and learn to trust that inner musical voice. In the end, we can rely only on what speaks inside of us, if the music is to be both spontaneous and believable. Any dishonesty about the origin of music will manifest itself in the tone of the choir. Their spirits will not be able to speak through the composer. Each of us must learn to trust and listen to our own musical instincts. It is from that trust and listening that great music making is born.
(James Jordan, Forward to *Evoking Sound, Second Edition*)

Every conducting experience is an opportunity not to be wasted.
(Ruben Alcala)

One could say, "You have not been in my classroom. I have to cheer-lead with exaggerated gestures." I believe strongly that I must train my people to respond to recognized gestures. This is most important when singing with an orchestra. Our gestures should focus on the music and notation and not detract from it. This means adjusting patterns to convey what, in your opinion, allows the composer's intentions to be realized.
(John Yarrington, *Choral Journal,* October, 2020)

I teach students to stand still, to let the sound come to them, to influence (evoke) every aspect with appropriate gesture, beginning with a breath-impulse that conveys meaning. If we don't breathe, they won't either. We breathe, however, with a body aligned, tall and spacious. Our hand position is curved and welcoming. We expect response. We command respect.

We do not, however, do "their" work. My students feel hindered, they tell me, by having to appropriate a spacious alignment. Instead, they want to express the music by moving, bobbing their head, hunching their shoulders, mouthing words and working much too hard. This picture reminds me of the circus performer spinning the plates. He runs to and fro, attempting to keep all plates spinning. Guess what? Some fall off.

Choir members, trained in a cheer-leading mentality, are not prepared for a professional conductor whose gesture conveys everything possible about the music. They must be trained. Those of us who teach must attempt to train the conductors in our charge to believe and to trust in those playing and singing. This is nothing akin to a vote, however. Nor is this a call for a structure-less or non-demanding rehearsal atmosphere. Rather, it IS a call for careful score study to know WHAT to conduct and refined gesture to show WHERE and HOW the music goes.

Our students should not mistake what is done on the podium by a famous orchestral conductor for effective gesture. For the most part, these are tremendously gifted individuals. One should attend a rehearsal to get the real substance of what can happen to an orchestra or choir in the hands of such an individual. Those of us who dwell in lower climes, however, should work toward making sure that nothing is shown which is not needed, and that we continue to reinforce the responsibility of the music makers in the project.

What can gesture accomplish? Gesture can establish tempo, create a breath full of all of the color and quality needed, evoke sound appropriate to the style, attract the music makers, set the tone and show line, direction, shape of words, destinations, dynamics, growth change. Gesture can reinforce softer-louder, *staccato, legato, marcato*, unaccented syllables, appropriate cues, elongating any beat for emphasis and phrase shapes.

The truth is, we can't make anyone play or sing a single note. We bring to bear everything we have learned about theory and harmony and form and style and history to inform and enliven the music making. Moreover, an attitude of community in the music making where individuals are cared for and honored is crucial. Singing is relational. There is a vast difference between seeking the utmost from a group, expecting a high level of pitch, tone, musicality, language, enthusiasm and understanding – creating an atmosphere where everyone contributes – as opposed to many situations where the primary element is not community through music, but rather an atmosphere of tension and fear of failure.

Alice Parker, in an editorial in her newsletter, *Melodious Accord*, March 2011, speaks of attending a lecture on Mind-Body Connections at the local Community College, ". . . which gave ma a new way to describe a chorus: it's a neurobiological system. This means that each individual is a part of the whole; each separate nervous system is connected to all the others. Our brains are not just 'tofu in the head,' but include our whole information-gathering body. And the body doesn't end with the finger-tips or toes: when we're in relationship with others, we are intimately connected into one nervous system. We feel not only our own emotional engagement, but are fed by all the others in the room. It's non-verbal communication at its best, with elements of meditation, of mindfulness, and of creating not only sound, but positive emotions."

Were I to write a letter to young conductors, it might say the following: I will expect you to eliminate all the excesses of gesture to which you are accustomed. Your strength is in clear, precise gestures that convey not just the technical demands of attack, release, dynamics, but the spirit and life of the music. This cannot be conveyed by your swaying and sweating, nor can you, yourself, sing or play the music. When you cross that line between conductor and chorus and orchestra, you jeopardize the result. You need to learn that less is more. You can control the sound, speed and shape of the music. You enable the music-making by receiving and molding the sound, always with gestures that unmistakenly convey what, in your judgment, the composer wants.

Your physical, aligned presence, in front of the group encourages their participation in the composer's intentions. Learn to stand tall, do not wiggle, sway, lean, stomp, or grunt. Work within your frame, using it as the backdrop for your gesture. Receive the sound – be in contact with it, but do not lean over to make someone play or sing. You should maintain poise and posture to command the respect and attention of the group. Your job is to train, encourage, enlighten and inspire, but not to get in their way. Your gestures, at once economical and effective, convey the sense and spirit of the music. Any unnecessary movement of frame or gesture weakens the result.

Learn to use a baton. Most of you will have occasion to conduct voices and instruments, from smaller ensembles to a full orchestra and the usual practice is to use a baton. You will be better served if you have a well-developed baton technique, so that you can choose what best serves the music. Orchestral players are skeptical of choral folk because, often, the choir has been trained in gestures known only to them. These special, secret signs baffle orchestral members who expect, when looking up, to see downbeats, clear cut-offs, basic patterns. Anything else results in a terrible waste of time and at worst, chaos!

Once a score is properly taught and marked by both singers and instrumentalists, your job is to enable the most musical, spirit-filled performance possible, attempting to represent the composer in his or her best light. Singers need precise indication as to attacks and releases, and reminders of subtleties of phrasing, articulation, and word shapes. You cannot make them do anything by sheer physical force. When you do, you get in the way of the music's unfolding and look foolish in the process. As for the competent instrumentalists, they usually do not need a dramatic conducting gesture from you. Often, an acknowledgment by looking in their direction will suffice. After sitting for 104 measures without playing, it is comforting to that person when a conductor gives a discreet cue with gesture or look to say: "Come in now, and welcome to the performance." If the proceedings run amok, if the group speeds up, slows down, plays too loudly, too softly, too legato, too staccato, your job is to regain control quickly and efficiently. At that point, you are the boss, the "maestro," and you are in charge. If your conducting "grammar" has been clear to this point, you have a chance for a save. Otherwise, good luck!

You are beginning to get the focus of this book: what is not efficient needs to be eliminated. Useless motion, twitching, swaying, hunching of shoulders, leaning over, gestures too large – any excess, no matter how learned or practiced, needs to be excised. New techniques feel uncomfortable at first: expect it! Also expect suggestions that run counter to what a previous teacher has said. Welcome the chance to try a new way. Then, you may decide with practice and experience which gestures and signals you will choose. Yarrington's Law: what do they need? More is wasteful!

Aligned posture gives to the conductor a sense of presence, a sense that the one on the podium is in charge and ready to lead. This is an unmistakable signal to singers and players. Another word is "presence." Even when nervous – especially when nervous – "assuming the pose" will help. As Wesley said, "Preach faith till you have it."

How then do we then take this grammar of conducting and apply it to every piece? Does our study of stylistic differences based on historical reference make a difference in our conducting? Asking questions of the particular piece is crucial: What kind of piece are you? Do you have any brothers or sisters? What else has this composer written? Listening to recordings, attending concerts, auditing rehearsals, are all ways to help you decide about appropriate tone, phrasing, articulation, tempo, balance, necessary performing forces and appropriate performance practice. Reading about music is one frame of reference. Learning from performance is also valuable. Do not wait until you direct the Chicago Symphony Chorus to begin this quest – start now!

In your conducting, is a real musical sense conveyed? Does your study and technique result in a performance which is musically convincing and rings true? "Dull" is a four-letter word which should be forever eliminated from the musical vocabulary. No choir has to sound dull and lifeless. That spark which ignites the great performances often comes from the inner spirit of the conductor as he or she guides and infuses a performance, at once accurate and musical. Investing in group responsibility for being part of the music making, plus the way in which you teach and pace the rehearsal, causes the singers to have a firm grasp of the various elements of the piece. Your willingness to experiment with sound, color, articulation, tempo and dynamics, along with the above, make for the possibility of an exciting performance.

IN PURSUIT OF MUSICAL EXCELLENCE

READER REFLECTIONS

7

Already Too Loud!

Understanding the World of the Orchestra

Understanding the role of the Conductor:
1) Understanding the world of the orchestra

> The relationship with a chorus is different than with an orchestra. It's closer, friendlier.
> -- (Student quote in *Voice of Chorus America* Volume 30, No. 1, Fall, 2006)

> There is not a choral conductor in a responsible college or university, a church which aspires to serve a discriminating congregation or a community arts program, who does not today come "face to face" with the great historical choral/orchestral literature – and "face to face" with instrumentalists and orchestras."
> -- (Robert Shaw, foreword to the first edition of *Face to Face With an Orchestra,* Indiana University Press)

> When the orchestra arrives to rehearse with the chorus in the last few days before a major performance, the mixture of musical cultures can be exhilarating and bewildering in unexpected ways."
> -- (Thomas Lloyd, *Choral Journal,* December, 1999)

One hires professional players who should be able to play

IN PURSUIT OF MUSICAL EXCELLENCE

what has been scheduled; but, if you have had little experience and do not understand the instrumental "mentality," you could be in for multiple shocks. The truth is, most of these players understand and play their instrument well.

If you study the score, mark parts, have a conference with the concertmaster (if strings are involved), conduct cleanly, ask specifically for what you want (shorter, longer, louder, softer, "*poco-legato*," "*poco-staccato*") and if you understand what singers must do to sing with an instrumental ensemble, you have a chance for a "good performance."
-- (John Yarrington)

2) Understanding the role of the conductor

A three year old, whom I know, always referred to me as "The Connector." Like many malapropisms, her delightful slip of the tongue reveals a lot. Conducting is all about connecting the composer and the musicians to the music and to the audience: and hope, by strengthening these links, you are a conductor in the specific sense of the term.
Mark Wigglesworth, *The Silent Musician*

To the question, "What weaknesses do you see in most choral conductors?" Margaret Hillis responded:

They need to learn to study a score properly and make contact with the sound. Sonority: there is the feeling that the sonority is in your hands and that the music itself goes right by your face. Some things about conducting cannot be taught. Talent cannot be taught. You cannot really teach group dynamics. There has to be a sense of the atmosphere and you have to know when to move on, when something has been rehearsed enough. I do demand detail, thinking, and connecting, but it

> has to be in the context of the whole.
> -- (An interview with Margaret Hillis – Dennis Keene, *Choral Journal,* January, 1992)

Why would someone pose the question: "Are you a choral conductor?"

Often, because of lack of knowledge or experience, with instrumental accompaniment, which might include brass quartet, string quintet, etc., the person on the podium conducts the choir and treats the "orchestra" as accompaniment rather than an integral part of the music making. I have seen on the stage well-prepared choirs using instrumental ensemble with no attention paid to the instrumentalists. One conductor NEVER looked at the instrumentalists!

LESS IS MORE

> The comic stereotype of an indulged megalomaniac, whose self-importance doesn't seem to match what the orchestra musicians are doing, is a pervasive cliché. The last person to enter the room . . . proceeds to perform a series of exaggerated gestures that vaguely coincide with the energy of the music . . .
>
> Contrary to some people's perception of conductors, it appears that in fact a monkey would not able to do a better job. Good news for the conductor. Bad news for the monkey.
>
> The more physical effort one puts in, the harder it is to listen properly The more you conduct, the less you hear. Franz Liszt usefully pointed out that conductors are steersmen, not oarsmen.
> -- (Mark Wigglesworth, *The Silent Musician*)

IN PURSUIT OF MUSICAL EXCELLENCE

> The origin of the need for a conductor lies in the most basic requirement for musicians to play or sing together, especially in circumstances, musicality or otherwise, where it might not be possible for them to hear each other well.
> -- (Patrick Summers, *The Spirit of this Place*)

In conducting classes at HBU, when I saw someone flailing about, swaying, grunting, mouthing, with gesture unclear, I would say to the class: "What is that called?" Their answer: "choral conducting."

Instrumentalists especially want to be part of excellence in performance. If the choir has been properly prepared, if the conductor understands all the ramifications of the "full" score, along with what to say and what not to say to the players, an inspired performance is possible on one rehearsal. It just isn't easy!

I am eternally grateful to Marge Cornelius, cello professor at the University of Oklahoma who helped me understand what it means to work with instrumentalists. I was fortunate in that church and in the others I served, to have the forces and the resources to do major works with orchestra. I recall working on the recitatives in the Bach *St. John Passion* which the McFarlin choir was presenting during Holy Week. Marge was patient but brutal in her criticisms of what I thought was clear. I always make my students conduct recitative.

At SMU, in a masters conducting class, I suggested that we conduct the tenor recitative, *No. 2*, from *Messiah*. I was horrified at what I saw in the beginning. The opening measures were subdivided in such a way that it was impossible to tell where the next measure began. As instrumentalists look at this, their initial impression is: "Choral Conductor!" We are all tarred with the same brush, unfortunately. After a time, these students were able to cleanly deliver what was necessary. They learned to show the shape of those first four eighth notes toward the quarter note on the third beat and to stop the stick when appropriate (as in measure four on beat two). Of course the terms *"senza rip,"* *"basso continuo,"* and *"con rip"* were literally foreign expressions.

How, then, does one become a "conductor" and not a "choral" conductor?

In *Face to Face with an Orchestra* (Second, expanded edition) authors, Don V. Moses, Robert W. Demaree, Jr., and Allen F. Ohmes help those of us trained as choral conductors to expand our horizons to include that wonderful paring of choir and orchestra. In the preface to the first edition, Robert Shaw observed: "Two things strike me as being very special about the book: first, it is remarkably efficient and practical. Second, in spite of its expertise and good counsel, it somehow manages to escape "authoritarianism." It invites, even "inspires" the reader's (conductor's) further study, exploration and individual creativity as regards performance practices and stylistic detail." -- (Robert Shaw in the Forward to *Face to Face with an Orchestra*)

It is not my intention to duplicate this material. I do, however, want to affirm the approach and also to state that I learned much of this the hard way and would love to have had the book earlier in my career. There are three parts: working with an orchestra, conducting three Baroque masterworks, conducting three Viennese Classical masterworks.

What I know is that much of the greatest music of the Western World is intended to be performed by chorus and orchestra. Many choral directors have limited experience in rehearsing and performing with orchestra. The demands upon the choir, for instance, in such a collaboration are distinctly different from a typical choral performance. Much has to be done with consonant articulation.

"Consonants are OUR bow-strokes." Often a choir, not used to singing with orchestra and not properly prepared, finds itself behind the beat. My choirs are always better after having had an experience with orchestra because they are more "on their game." I also grow as a conductor.

My students will remark: "Dr. Yarrington, you make it look so easy." A nice compliment, but without understanding the hours of score study, marking, and the terror I usually feel upon ascending the podium. There is so much sound coming at you! Once I am there, and have done my work, I really enjoy the process. Actually, I enjoy the rehearsal more than the performance because I love seeing what happens when instrumentalists perceive that the conductor knows what to do- what to say and what not to say- and the choir has been prepared well.

I say to singers: once the orchestra hears that you sing well, in tune, accurately, rhythmically, they automatically play better. Can this happen on ONE rehearsal? Most of the time, for me, it does . . . and can! It just takes an enormous amount of work.

> To quote the authors in *Face to Face with an Orchestra*:
> "Accustomed to the nature and the special techniques of choral work, we may find it strange to deal instead with the expectations and needs of instrumentalists. Working with amateur players, we may not be able to help them enough; working in turn with professionals, we may feel intimidated. In either case, we find ourselves unable to achieve our best intentions." (p. 3)

The problem is not with the players. Most of it can be eliminated by preparation, precise language and experience. To confront an orchestra with confidence, one first must understand as much as possible about the instruments, the musicians, and their standard ways of communicating with each other.

My checklist is as follows:

1. Score study obviously. Those of us who do not work with instrumentalists on a regular basis must prepare. I believe in the use of recordings to help in this process. The danger is in taking someone else's interpretation, *tempi*, etc. However, it is most helpful and I encourage my students to watch and listen only to the orchestral part, then only to the choral part, and then listen to the

whole. This represents much time and effort and concentration. If one watches the score listening to only one section at a time, concentrating on just winds, or strings, the cumulative effect is to begin to understand how that section contributes to the whole.

2. Eye contact from the podium, AHEAD of entrances is crucial. If your gesture comes at the same time as their entrance, they don't need you. Will they come in without you? Most likely they will. If, however, you never look or "invite" them into the performance they may think that you are a.............?

3. In the conducting be clear: good preparations, downbeats, indication of articulation, dynamics, change of *tempi*. Don't talk!

4. Have a seating chart with the names of the players. You can then ask: "Marilyn, could we have a bit more second oboe there." Marilyn is NOT a second oboe. She PLAYS second oboe.

5. Don't stop. Play through so the players know what is involved. One of the hardest things to teach a young conductor is that, many times, mistakes will be corrected the second time through. It is important to keep going, even if it is, at first, rather rough. It will get better but not if you stop all the time or talk excessively.

6. Let them play. It is wasteful to adjust balances between choir and orchestra in a first run-through. When the players experience the whole, they will be more aware of the needs of balance. I am sure everyone does this, but I often ask just the orchestra to play so the choir can listen and vice-versa. Our tendency is to ask the orchestra to play softer when often we need better consonant articulation from the choir. Asking the orchestra to play shorter, not to unnecessarily prolong long notes, or even to play into their stands works wonders. First, LET THEM PLAY. Then, be specific: shorter, longer, *diminuendo* on longer notes, louder, softer. The choir must have an instrumental mentality. They must anticipate entrances, add voices (choral orchestration) when necessary, listen, contribute and always be just a bit ahead of the stick.

7. I find it helpful to have specific reference points, especially in a longer work. When I stop I need to know exactly where to go. Nothing defuses a wonderful rehearsal quicker than the conductor's hemming and hawing around about where to start. We also must examine the parts to see if either numbers or letters or both are the same as in the full score and choral parts. Less experienced conductors should look at the individual parts from which instrumentalists play. For a choral person, it is as if one had ONLY the soprano part or ONLY the alto part. Singers are spoiled because we essentially see a full score. It is a delightful experience, in a conducting class, to give only the soprano part to the sopranos, alto part, etc., and ask everyone to sing. Most revealing.
8. Use a known contractor who hires the players for you. This person is your best friend because he/she knows who "plays well together." This will not be an ensemble that regularly plays together. If, however, you have done your work, they will play wonderfully for you. Everyone wants to be in a successful performance. You have to help.
9. Seating the orchestra may require some changes, especially in a church situation where you are not able, because of physical constraints, to arrange them in a more or less traditional set-up. Again, your contractor can help you with this. When you know the seating, part of your preparation is to practice conducting and looking at the right folks at the right time.
10. The concert master is also your best friend. A session with that person pays big dividends. Also, deferring to that person in the rehearsal speeds things along. I may seem like time wasted, but it never is.

A number of our graduates were going out to high school jobs or church jobs or both. Working with amateur singers is more than worthwhile – is life changing and life giving! To the man in one of my choirs who said that the final chorus in the Bach *St. John Passion* was the most wonderful moment in his life, I say: that's what it's all about. Loving the singers, loving the process, attaining the product. That we care about "them" is as important as the product itself.

In the Massachusetts ACDA *Choral News*, outgoing president, Joshua R. Jacobson, espouses making music collegially: "Music is basic to the human condition. Our job, as conductors, is to help people do what comes naturally: to select, refine and polish: to organize, enable and encourage. We're not asking anyone to perform an unnatural act! So why do we often find ourselves in the position of taskmaster and disciplinarian, imposing our will on a reluctant ensemble or audience? Do we dominate our choirs for the sake of an artistic product, or to fortify our egos? Challenge your singers to become more musically self-reliant; they need not abdicate all responsibility to the conductor. Demonstrate that you trust their sensitivity. Consider even allowing your large choirs to perform in concert without the constant domination of a conductor.

JUST FOR FUN CONDUCTOR QUOTES:

"I'd like to talk to Brahms about that. Maybe he'll write me a letter."

"I haven't got all day, turn the page faster or we'll have to pass out refreshments."

"There is a difference between soft and scared."

"You can go ahead and practice this work – it won't hurt."

"If you rush that spot, we'll get to a tempo even God couldn't play."

-- (Dr. Robert Linder, former Dean of the School of Music at HBU, conductor of the Houston Civic Orchestra and the Gilbert and Sullivan Orchestra.)

"I purposely didn't do anything and you were all behind."

"Watch me closely. Only one can spoil it."

"Brass: stay down all summer."

"We can't hear the balance because the soloist is still on the airplane."

"Percussion a little louder." (We don't have anything.)
"That's right. Play it louder."
-- (Eugene Ormandy)

JOHN YARRINGTON

READER REFLECTIONS

8

The Relationship Quotient

Being yourself is more important than being who you
think people might want you to be. Even though you
might have to highlight some aspects of your character
more than others, you are who you are. Better to adjust
the volume than twirl the dial in search of another channel.
-- (Peter Loel Boonshaft, *Teaching Music with Passion*,
Meredith Music Publications-GW Music)

The benefits of a conductor sharing the responsibility
for musicality entrances with the instrumentalists are significant
on a human level as well as a musical level. Our relationship
with the musicians should equal to our relationship to the music.

We have a duty to lead the morale of the group.
Creating and maintaining a positive morale is where
the musical and human qualities of a conductor meet.
-- (Mark Wigglesworth, *The Silent Musician*)

When asked, "Do you think all any of us really want,
deep down, is to be loved?" Garrison Keillor responded:
"No, we want to be rich, to be admired, to eat like a horse and
be skinny as a snake. To have small children ask for our
autographs, to be on terrific medications that make us calm
and witty and sexy. To sing Irving Berlin and Gershwin and

Porter at *The Room* and be described in the *Times* as 'luminous.' But in the absence of all that, it's enough to be loved." (Salon.com)

> To laugh often and much, to win the respect of intelligent people and the affection of children, to earn the appreciation of honest critics and endure the betrayal of false friends, to appreciate beauty, to find the best in others, to leave the world a bit better, whether by a healthy child, a garden patch . . . to know even one life has breathed easier because you have lived. This is to know you have succeeded.
> -- (Ralph Waldo Emerson, quoted on p. 16 of *The Musician's Spirit,* James Jordan)

"What I am I must become" is the title of a poem by Nancy Wood, based on the Hopi tradition. It's been haunting my mind for the last few weeks as I work on a commissioned piece for the Amherst Middle School – it seems to apply not only to these young teens in their fine chorus, but to me as well. Who are we? What are we becoming? Do we see and hear beauty around us? Do we honor our own feelings and those of others? Do we feel the interdependence when we sing in a group? Are we newly energized by creating choral sound? Can we base our lives and our daily behavior and our music making in this perception-that we really are one people, one human race, and that our purpose is not only to create beauty but to reflect it around us? What I am I must become. Indeed."
-- (Alice Parker, in the *Melodious Accord Newsletter,* March, 2011, p. 3)

"Mr. President, I understand you have been a church choir singer." His fact lit up, and he replied, "You know, I started singing in choirs when I was eight years old.

IN PURSUIT OF MUSICAL EXCELLENCE

It has always been a very important part of my life."
-- (President Bill Clinton, *Choral Journal*, Vol. 32, Number 11, p. 20, June and July, 2012)

"Singing is Relational": This is on the board at the beginning of every choir year.
-- (John Yarrington)

As conductors, understanding and acceptance of our equal role with singers is a prerequisite to great music making at any level. We actually do not conduct; we "evoke" sounds from our singers with our gesture, which is set in motion with our own breath – the miracle that is the musical phrase. After that, we guide singers not with our hands but with our ears. It is our responsibility as conductors to intimately understand which gestures help singers and which gestures hinder singers and cause the music not to sing.
-- (James Jordan in *Evoking Sound*)

You know you have been around for awhile . . . when you are asked to clinic a youth choir and one of the sponsors is a "youth" who sang with you in Norman, Oklahoma, and his son is in this choir! The father shows me a postcard which he has saved. It has a mimeographed (that dates me) message which went to everyone in the choir but with an added personal note to him from me. He has saved this all these years! Looking back, I realize that I almost always added a personal note to any correspondence that went out in the churches.

This brings home a truth: everyone who sings has special qualities and to acknowledge those personally is a vital part of what I do. Who of us does not like to receive a personal word? In our cyber-society with email and *Facebook* and the like so prevalent, we can lose sight of this important ingredient. How long does it take to write a couple of sentences? Not long! How important is this? Vital!

To stand in front a group of singers or instrumentalists is to be vulnerable. To ask them to join you in a wonderful journey of music making is part of the equation which allows everyone to participate. My struggle has always been that I am not "tough" enough. I have come to the realization that our work is not about "tough" but about "care." My careful study and preparation allows me to step on the podium and lead in a disciplined, creative, loving way, always asking for the best from everyone in the room. My church choirs and my students will tell you that I am exacting in what I expect and will settle for no less than the best. Not every rehearsal, however, is a shining moment. Sometimes we must slog through the mud to get there. At HBU we had a rehearsal which began with what I called, "weed-eating" – you know, to cut out the weeds. Everyone was expected to sing his/her own part in front of the group – no quartets – no help. This way, the responsibility is shared and everyone knows who is pulling weight and who is a slacker. The students told me that practice rooms were full for several nights before the actual weed-eating experience. In every rehearsal to this day, I expect everyone to mark carefully – marking being a "sign of intelligence." Often, I become frustrated but I do not take that frustration out on the group in demeaning ways. Great music is not made out of fear.

However, in the car on the way home from the Presbyterian choir rehearsal, my wife, who is my best supporter and fiercest critic, will say: "The way you looked at that soprano – you could have bitten her head off." My response was: "I didn't mean that." My wife rejoined: "But the bite marks are still there." She often says to me about the church choir: "Honey, they are doing the best they can." My response is: "It's not GOOD enough."

But we come back another day, don't we?

My student, Ruben Alcala, was the first recipient of the John Yarrington Fellowship in Choral Conducting which provided a scholarship for an aspiring conducting student.

From someone who had very little conducting experience, he developed into one of the finest conducting students I have ever taught. It was a pleasure to watch him grow. I was able to give him more and more responsibility for rehearsal and performance and he always proved worthy of the experience.

Following are excerpts from a letter I wrote to him when he applied to graduate school which I believe states well my philosophy. When I am tempted to doubt my ability or to beat on myself because I am not as good as . . . or as tough as . . . I remember these words of wisdom I attempted to convey to Ruben. They sum up what I believe about me as well:

Dear Ruben,

When I think about your going to these auditions for grad school, I am reminded of the conducting seminar I attended with Dr. Julius Herford, Robert Shaw's teacher. I was on the podium in front of singers and orchestra, with Dr. Herford and others sitting at a table WATCHING. It felt a bit like a picture of a religious inquisition. I learned then, what I know now and have tried to impart to you.

I have to do what I do best without regard to those watching. For me, this is hard, because my tendency is to compare myself to others, even though I know what I do is plenty good enough.

Do others have better singers? In lots of instances, yes. Are others smarter? Hate to admit it, but, yes. After all these years, rehearsals, workshops, articles, books, I think I may finally be at a point, however, where I really do "what I know" and let the chips fall.

I love working with students. Sometimes, the way I work is misinterpreted as a kind of weakness, because I don't turn over chairs or "call people out." I believe, as you know, in a sacred quality of kinship with the people I conduct. I care deeply about them. I think that the best music is always made in an atmosphere of community. I know that there are those who take advantage, but those folks always do that anyway. Some are always looking for a shortcut. My job is to take what I have and do the best I know with it. I can't do anything else.

In all of this, awareness of one's self – acceptance of strengths and weaknesses – a non-comparing attitude of constantly learning, refining, listening, making progress gives one the satisfaction of a job well done. The "comparison game" is energy wasted. I know that! Still, I indulge. I am my own worst critic and often fail to value my strengths because I am so focused on my weaknesses. I am surely not alone.

In our own sphere of influence, we should study hard and love much. To value the music but not value the music makers is a mistake. We discipline (vowels, consonants, articulation) out of love but in such a positive atmosphere that every singer or player is valued, celebrated and appreciated. I have been blessed both in church and school to have had some of the most wonderful personal relationships any man could have. I have students who swear by me. I have some who swear AT me. Many a volunteer singer in one of the volunteer church choirs I have directed has sung in a manner he or she never dreamed possible. They have sung music that was hard, exacting, often with orchestra, and lived to tell about it.

I am grateful beyond measure for all of this. I often tell people that there have been very few days in all these years that I have not gotten up with anticipation for what I was going to do: make music I love with people I love. Truly, it doesn't get better than this.

I leave you with a quote from my friend, Jim Jordan:

> Conducting is a creative act. Musical creativity requires faith – almost blind faith in one's ear and one's inner musical voice. Implicit in that blind faith is a requirement to relinquish control of both the music and others. Regardless of a conductor's depth of musical background, the steps into a creative life as a conductor require trust in self and others. When that path is followed, profound music is made.
> -- (James Jordan in *Evoking Sound*, p. 7)

READER REFLECTIONS

9

Why Making Music Matters

We live in community and song is a language that unites us
more surely than any made up of words.
It is the language of the heart-we teach love when we sing.
-- (Alice Parker *Melodius Accord*, July, 2007)

"*Owmwani ni wa bhone Omwana*: It Takes a Village to
Raise a Child."

This is the text of that song which the First Presbyterian Choir sang on our recent tour of the Holy Land:

"Oh Children, sing out! Everybody sing it strong—in praise
of the village where all belong. Oh Children, sing out!
Sing it clear together we nurture all children here.
Oh Families, sing it strong—in praise of the village where
all belong—together we cherish all families here.
And many villages make a nation, many
nations make a global home."

Here are three snapshots to illustrate the importance of making music and how it happens:
PERLMAN MAKES HIS MUSIC—THE HARD WAY
(*Houston Chronicle*, February 10, 2021)

IN PURSUIT OF MUSICAL EXCELLENCE

On Nov. 18, Itzhak Perlman, the violinist, came on stage to give a concert at Lincoln Center in New York City.

Perlman was stricken with polio as a child, and just getting on stage is no small achievement. He has braces on both legs and walks painfully and slowly to reach his destination. He sits down, puts the crutches on the floor, he undoes the clasps on his leg braces. Th audience is used to this—they wait—after a few bars a string breaks—the audience thought another violin was to be brought out—instead, he waited a moment and began playing where he left off.

Everyone knows that it is impossible to play a symphonic work with three strings—Perlman refused to know this. He continued, changing, reharmonizing, modulating. After he finished, the crowd roared with loud cheers. He raised his bow and said, "You know, sometimes it is the artist's task to find how much music you can still make with what you have left."

Perhaps this is a definition of life: not just for artists but for all of us. Perhaps in this shaky, fast-moving, bewildering world in which we live, our task is to make music at first with all we have and then, when that is no longer possible, to make music with what we have left.

STUDENT VIOLINIST PLAYS SONG OF PERSEVERANCE WITH BOW ATTACHMENT
(*Houston Chronicle*)

Kevin Vasquez's father instilled in him a love for song before he died in a motorcycle accident when Kevin was only four years old. When Kevin is sad, he sings. At age ten, in the fifth grade, Kevin was allowed to choose an elective. Drawn to music, he chose a violin class. Because he was born without a left hand, he and his mother doubted that he would ever be able to play along with his classmates. His violin teacher, Mary Fimble, searched the internet and found another boy who also was missing his left hand but was able to play the violin with an apparatus. The website provided guidance to recreate the device. After over one hundred fifty hours of volunteer work and many trials and errors, Kevin was presented with this device—strips of thermal plastic produced by a 3D printer. He played! More adjustments will need to be made but for Kevin, "All my wishes are coming true!"

LESSON IN HUMANITY FROM A MASTER
(*New York Times*, January, 1994)

I was privileged to be one of one hundred singers from all over the world to participate in a week-long seminar sponsored by Carnegie Hall, with Robert Shaw. The piece to be performed was the Britten *War Requiem*. Shaw spoke with feeling to the chorus about joining the text of the *Requiem Mass* for the dead, with the anti-war poetry of Wilfred Owens, who was killed in World War l. Said Mr. Shaw, "The chorus is getting quite good—this is an extraordinary chorus—I don't know its equal anywhere in the world and it is two and a half days old." The intensity of this week-long workshop with Mr. Shaw is hard to describe. We were preparing for a concert in Carnegie Hall on the following Sunday. Benjamin Luzon was to sing the very important baritone solo, which he had performed before with Mr. Shaw. Unfortunately, he had gone almost totally deaf in recent years because of a problem with his immune system. His left ear failed in March, 1991, and his right ear was attacked as well. Said Mr. Luxon, "Nothing wrong with my stupid voice—taking steroids and chemo to slow down deterioration—no feeling of projection—having to relearn to use my voice." In the two full run-throughs of the piece at the Manhattan Center, Mr. Luzon, who is prone to sharpness, but refuses to play it safe, entered high by a good margin in the concluding "Let us sleep now." Both times he realized his problem and shook his head in exasperation. What suddenly became obvious was that Mr. Shaw had invited a bull into his china shop. He put all of that painstaking preparation at risk because, he said, "Mr. Luzon brings a human quality to the piece that I have never heard anywhere else." Said Mr. Shaw before the performance, "The aesthetics and the modification of social behavior that come from a love of beauty and from the disciplines of accomplishment, are terribly important to our civilization, especially in a society where both religion and political organizations have abdicated their responsibilities for human change."

I came home a changed person. What a wonderful experience.

I have always loved this quote from Ralph Vaughn Williams and it seems an appropriate work with which to close this chapter and this book:

"As long as a country is content to take its music passively, there can be no really artistic vitality in the nation. In England, we tend to speak in terms of the Queens Hall and Covent Garden. They are, so to speak, the crest of the wave. But behind that wave must be the driving force which makes up the body of the wave. It is below the surface that we look for the power which occasionally throws up a Schanble, a Sibelius, or Toscanni. What makes me hope for the musical future of any country is not the distinguished names which appear on the front page of the newspapers, but the music that is going on at home, in the schools, and in the local choral societies." -- (Used by Permission)

JOHN YARRINGTON

READER REFLECTIONS

EPILOGUE

In an article entitled, "Remembering Robert Shaw," (*Melodious Accord Newsletter*, March, 1999), Alice Parker writes about her experience over many years with Mr. Shaw:

> What did I learn? There's no holding back – throw yourself in, without counting the cost or time. Be your own harshest critic (I was never as good at that as he). Listen all the time: the specific word, accent, mouth, voice, person, composer. Capture the sound on the page. In the last analysis (and the first) one can't separate the text, the melody and the setting: it's all one. In study and rehearsal, one pulls them apart, but only to re-unite them. I learned that the spirit is in the details. That sharing ideas, bouncing them back and forth, is enormous fun, stimulating both players to greater achievement. That almost anything can be improved. That one is walking a delicate balance-line between thought and action, intuition and craft, rehearsal and performance, life and art. And that music is one of the greatest gifts. And sternest masters. When we enter its world, we must submerge our individuality in its surge and ebb, only finding our own voice through the mastery of its demands. It's a lot to live up to.
>
> Thanks, Robert, and rest well.

My musical life has been shaped by these two: Alice Parker and Robert Shaw. Listening to those wonderful recordings of the Robert

EPILOGUE

Shaw Chorale formed my idea of choral sound, beauty and balance. Fifty years of studying with Alice Parker has helped me understand what music is all about – the importance of text - the commitment to excellence, the joy of being prepared and the asking of simple questions about a song: "What kind of song are you? Do you have brothers and sisters? How might you sound in your most habitable environment?"

Alice would sing to us in those sessions in New York and we would try to match the inflection and mood of what she sang. Often failing. She would ask again in an inviting manner and keep at it until we got closer. I have seen her take a large group of people and have them singing and enjoying it – without accompaniment always encouraging, continuing to demonstrate, never scolding. This is at the bedrock of my own teaching.

So I would say, "It's a lot to live up to, Alice. Thrive and live. You are loved."

I want to recommend three books by Peter Loel Boonshaft: *Teaching Music with Passion* (conducting, rehearsing and inspiring), *Teaching Music with Promise* and *Teaching Music with Purpose*. Boonshaft says, "The phrase I always think of when it comes to pedagogy is: 'Why is it that there is never enough time to do things right . . . but always enough time to do them over."

It seems only appropriate, to quote Maestro Shaw in closing. This is from an address given at the University of Oklahoma, November 19, 1977, and unpublished:

> There's no easy-on-easy-off for Truth. There's no landscaped approach to Beauty. You scratch and scramble around intellectual granites; you try to defuse or tether your emotional tantrums; you pray for the day when your intellect and your instinct can co-exist, that the brain need not calcify the heart, nor the heart o'er flood and drown all reason. But in the struggle lies dignity and a tolerable

EPILOGUE

destiny. (The alternatives to life aren't all that attractive anyway.) So while we're here, lets hold fast to the liberating, conserving, arts. -- For man in his available glory is clothed only by such as these.

- And without them there soon could be no body to clothe.

EPILOGUE

READER REFLECTIONS

BIBLIOGRAPHY

Barr, Cameron and Wykoff, John. THE MELODIC VOICE. Chicago: GIA Publications, Inc., 2019.

Jordan, James and Whitbourn, James. THE MUSICIAN'S TRUST. Chicago: GIA Publications, Inc., 2013

Jordan, James and Thomas, Nova. TOWARD CENTER. Chicago: GIA Publications, Inc., 2010.

Melodious Accord Newsletter. Hawley, MA: Melodious Accord, Inc.

Parker, Alice. THE ANATOMY OF MELODY. Chicago: GIA Publications, Inc., 2006.

Summers, Patrick. THE SPIRIT OF THIS PLACE. Chicago: The University of Chicago Press, 2018.

Wigglesworth, Mark. THE SILENT MUSICIAN. London: Faber and Faber Limited, 2018.

Yarrington, John. HAVE WE HAD THIS CONVERSATION. The Woodlands, TX: Schott Bradshaw, Publications, LLC, 2008.

THE AUTHOR

John Yarrington, Professor in Music, Houston Baptist University, retired, currently is adjunct faculty in the Sacred Music Program at the University of St Thomas. He directs the Chancel Choir of the First Presbyterian Church of Houston and continues to teach private voice. Yarrington is no stranger to pedagogical publishing; his most recent publication being *Have We Had This Conversation*.

Dr. John Yarrington
- Choral Music
Professor,
Pedagogue / Author
*PENIEL UNLIMITED,
LLC*

www.ingramcontent.com/pod-product-compliance
Lightning Source LLC
Chambersburg PA
CBHW051457290426
44109CB00016B/1791